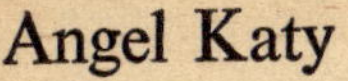
Angel Katy

GW01605549

Leah Harrow

Angel Katy

DRAGON
GRANADA PUBLISHING
London Toronto Sydney New York

Published by Granada Publishing Limited
in Dragon Books 1979

ISBN 0 583 30372 2

A Dragon Original

By arrangement with the British Broadcasting Corporation. The explosion incident referred to on pp. 50–51 was created for the BBC TV series by Alan Janes.

Granada Publishing Limited
Frogmore, St Albans, Herts AL2 2NF
and
3 Upper James Street, London W1R 4BP
866 United Nations Plaza, New York, NY 10017, USA
117 York Street, Sydney, NSW 2000, Australia
100 Skyway Avenue, Rexdale, Ontario, M9W 3A6, Canada
PO Box 84165, Greenside, 2034 Johannesburg, South Africa
CML Centre, Queen & Wyndham, Auckland 1, New Zealand

Made and printed in Great Britain by
Richard Clay (The Chaucer Press) Ltd
Bungay, Suffolk
Set in Linotype Times

For Julia, Tony and Ray.

1

Katy came off duty at four-thirty, and for the next half hour sat limply in the canteen with her feet propped up on an unoccupied chair. She had managed to find a table in line with a draught from the door and couldn't bear to leave it, so she sat on, long after her tea was finished, feeling sorry for her own hot self and for her poor aching feet, over there on the other side of the table.

Now and again she looked at her watch and promised herself another few minutes before she got up to face the walk home to the airless flat, along the fiery pavements, so it was well after five o'clock before she felt able to set her feet on the ground again. If she had had any foresight she would have brought along her sandals to walk home in. If she hadn't slept late this morning and left home in her usual panic, she would have brought a change of clothes and might have left the hospital feeling cool and clean instead of grubby and sticky and a whole stone heavier in her wilting uniform and dour black shoes that had surely become a size smaller since this morning.

The shoes felt unusually ventilated as she walked towards the gate and when she looked down she discovered that the left one was springing open at the toe. A sinister smile had appeared between the sole and the upper. Katy leaned against the bonnet of the nearest parked car and examined the damage. If anything, the right shoe was in worse health than the left. The sole was split right across, revealing some kind of interior that looked suspiciously like cardboard. The heels on both sloped steeply because she tended to walk on the outside of her feet.

She would have to buy a new pair.

She sat on the bonnet and swore.

Last week she had spent an entire afternoon buying new shoes, and enjoyed every minute of it, cruising from shop to shop and trying on the most unlikely and the most uncomfortable – and the most expensive – before going back for the first pair in the first shop, which was all she dared to afford. However, they had not been the kind of shoes that she could wear on the ward. She had danced in them on Saturday night. She grudged every moment, and every penny, spent on shoes for work, but this pair would scarcely hold together till she got home. They would never tread the floors of Casualty again. She set off once more, walking with extreme care.

There had been a girl in Casualty that afternoon who had severely damaged the semi-lunar cartilage in her knee by falling off her own shoes. Even allowing for the fact that she was badly shaken, she hadn't been very bright. Katy had to tell her that an operation might be necessary, explaining the meniscectomy in some detail, but when she left, the patient had been yelling at her boyfriend, 'She says I've got to have the cartridge took out,' so that all those waiting outside the cubicle probably imagined that someone had shot her.

With a voice like that, someone should, Katy thought.

The girl in Casualty had bright orange streaks in her hair. The streaks had not been altogether successful for she looked rather as if she had stood underneath something that dripped, but the cut had been good and Katy began to wonder, not for the first time, if she should have her own hair cut. No more hairpins puncturing her scalp; no more loose ends escaping from under her cap; no more precious time spent in putting it up when she could be asleep for another five minutes. But long hair was nicer to dance in.

The shop next to the tobacconist had changed hands again. It was one of those shops that never stayed the same six months together. Since Katy had first known it, it had been a florist's, a gents' outfitter, a reject china shop and a cut-price record bar. In between, the charities had it; Help the Aged, or Save the Children. Last time Katy looked it had been the Salvation Army, now it was a hairdresser's. Instead of finding the window full of old woollies and willow-pattern plates that didn't quite match Katy realized that she was looking straight into the salon, and the customers could look straight out into the street, secure in the knowledge that the whole of Battersea could see them in rats' tails and curlers, cotton wool and rollers or plastered with half-baked henna and half-baked themselves, under the drier.

Katy studied the price list. It seemed that you could no longer simply have your hair cut. For four pounds you could have it restyled. For five pounds you could have it remodelled, and this was just for starters. Katy was about to move on when an arm reached over the central display of dried, dyed and restyled pampas grass, and a hand in a rubber glove tapped on the window.

She looked along the arm and saw a face that she recognized at the other end of it. It was Elaine Bryant, who had come after Katy on the register at school and had been her best friend from time to time. They ceased to be friends in the fifth year when they discovered that they were both after the same bloke and Katy had won. Katy recalled the bloke in question and imagined that someone less fussy had him now. At any rate, she hadn't seen anything of Elaine since before she started at St Angela's and now, here was Elaine looking friendly again, waving her rubber hand, mouthing and nodding towards the door. Katy walked back to meet her.

'I thought it was you,' said Elaine, opening the door. 'I saw you go by a couple of times last week but you never looked up and I had somebody's head in the basin. You in a hurry?'

Katy, forgetting the shoes and remembering what awaited her at home, shook her head.

'Fancy finding you here. It's only just opened, hasn't it?'

'Couple of weeks ago.'

'You work here?'

'What do you think?' Elaine glanced over her shoulder and yelled, 'All right. I'm coming. I'm coming! Look, I'm off in ten minutes. D'you want a coffee? I'll meet you in that place round the corner with the dead cat in the window.'

'It's not dead.'

'I've never seen it move. All right. *Coming!*'

The door closed again. Katy walked on to the coffee bar where the manageress's striped tom lay curled up in the window between the gateaux, looking unpleasantly dead, now she came to think about it. Elaine, wherever she had been for the last three years, seemed to be doing all right for herself. That short meeting had been enough to show that the clothes she wore for work must cost at least twice as much as anything that Katy kept for best; and over the stinging chemical smell of the salon she had detected a perfume that certainly hadn't been picked up off the cosmetic counter at Woolworth's.

Elaine's ten minutes were nearer twenty before she arrived laden with a leather shoulder bag the size of an overnight case and several carrier bags, one of which was the flat plastic kind, made especially for holding LPs.

'I don't have to ask what you're doing with yourself, do

I?' said Elaine, shedding her load all over the bench seat. 'Unless that's fancy dress, I don't think. I thought you were going to be an air hostess.'

'I changed my mind, didn't I?' said Katy, trying to read the name on the record sleeve, through the thin plastic of the carrier.

'Aren't you matron yet, then?'

'Come off it. I'm only in my third year. You can't start training until you're eighteen. I worked in the council crèche at first. Don't you remember?'

'Ugh. Babies,' said Elaine. 'Two white coffees please, Missus, and a slice of that tabby cake you got in the window – you want another coffee, don't you? You must be barmy, nursing. Babies and stiffs and everything that's horrible in between. I don't know how you stick it.'

Since this was more or less what everybody said, Katy saved herself the bother of answering.

'Where've you been, then?' she said.

'Gravesend,' said Elaine. 'I went to work for my cousin. Well, you need to move about, don't you? See life.'

'In Gravesend?'

'You know what they tell you down there, don't you? They say it got its name during the Plague. There were these rows of graves, see, stretching down from London, and they built Gravesend at the end of them. I could believe it, too, after six months.'

'You been back long?'

'Ages,' said Elaine.

'Whyn't you come and see me, then?'

'Don't you live in the hospital?'

'Oh yes. Where, down the boiler room?' She searched for her purse.

'Have the coffee on me,' said Elaine, magnificently. 'I thought you'd be in a hostel or something. Bolts on the door, spikes on the wall, no pets, no fellas. In by ten or you get the boot in the morning.'

'That was about three hundred years ago,' said Katy. 'We've moved on a bit since then. Anyway, you have to do a sight worse than come home late to get kicked out. We're so short-staffed —'

'Well, where are you living then?' said Elaine, losing interest as soon as things turned out to be better than she expected. She was the kind who thought that hospital life was one long haemorrhage.

'I'm still at home,' said Katy.

'What! That hole over the shop? How d'you stick it?'

'Thanks very much, try saying that when my mum's around. It's not that bad – well, it wasn't until Gran moved in.'

'You think that's trouble? We've got my sister and her husband *and* the baby. They're supposed to be here on holiday, mind you, but it's no holiday.'

'*You're* still living at home then?' said Katy, swiftly. 'Ten flights up and the lift always broken. How d'you stick it?'

'Because the end's in sight, that's how,' said Elaine, smugly. She waggled her fingers. On one was an engagement ring.

'Nice,' said Katy, turning cautious. The conversation was likely to become sticky from here on, if she didn't watch out.

'*And* good. He's a company director.'

'A what? What company?' Katy imagined Marks & Spencer or ICI.

'*Lots* of companies,' said Elaine, vaguely. 'I dunno. I don't ask. Let's have another coffee – gor! Aren't you slow?'

'I have to make them last.'

'Well, drink up, I'm paying,' said Elaine. 'What about you, then? I suppose you're going to marry a doctor, ho ho.'

'I'm engaged to one – if you want to know,' said Katy.

'You're not!' Elaine looked as if she might be good for two minutes' silence after all.

'I am.'

'Let's see your ring, then.' Elaine twiddled her own ring, so that it caught the light.

'I don't wear it to work. You can only wear a wedding ring on duty.'

'You should hang it round your neck so you can get at it when you want it. My mum used to do that. She got engaged while she was still at school. When's the big day then?' Katy shrugged, but Elaine didn't give herself time to notice. 'We're getting married in October. D'you want to make it a double wedding?'

Katy tried to visualize Hughie in a morning suit, standing at the altar alongside a bent company director. 'If you don't mind waiting.'

'Oh. It's like that, is it?'

'No, it isn't,' said Katy. 'We've both got our careers to think of. I've got my finals this year and I have to apply for a job, for afterwards. Suppose I can't get anywhere local, Hughie won't – can't —'

'That's his name, is it? Hugh-eeee,' said Elaine, trying it out. 'What sort of a doctor is he?'

'Psycho.'

'A *loony*?'

'A psychiatrist,' said Katy, patiently, aware that not everyone thought this was an admirable thing to be.

'Oh, a loony doctor. Couldn't you find a normal one?'

'He is normal,' said Katy. 'You know what they say;

nurses marry doctors or policemen or firemen. They never meet anyone else.'

'Patients?'

'Not if they've got any sense.'

'Porters?'

'Oh...'

'They're people, aren't they?' said Elaine, surprisingly sharp.

'Yes, but —'

'But not quite people enough for nurses, I suppose. My brother's a porter; Malcolm. You remember him, don't you?'

'I've never noticed him,' said Katy, dismayed. How could she have missed him? Malcolm Bryant was the nearest thing to the Incredible Hulk that she had ever seen on the public highway.

'Oh, he's not in your manor,' said Elaine. 'He's at Wandsworth. Don't worry, you won't find *him* chasing you down the corridor one dark night.'

2

She had Tuesday and Wednesday off, and immediately the fine weather collapsed in a rainstorm that refused to die an easy death and lingered on in showers and wet winds until Wednesday evening. Thursday began in sunshine and by mid-day the tarnished trees that drooped along the street at intervals, revived and glittered like springtime. Katy glared ungratefully at them from the doorway of the shop. She was due to start on night shift that evening, which meant going to bed right now, after lunch, and drawing the curtains on the shining street.

When she got up again the sun was sliding down through a red sky, towards the railway arches, and she walked to the hospital full of self-pity, rehearsing the way in which she would have liked to spend this tender evening, walking with Hughie through the park to see the sun set from Albert Bridge, and then over the river to his favourite Chelsea pub which combined his twin enthusiasms of real ale and live jazz. Unfortunately there was a pub at Richmond that offered the same attractions and also the excuse of a high-speed journey in Hughie's Triumph Spitfire.

She had nothing against the pub at Richmond, and she enjoyed being seen in the Spitfire, but by the time they arrived the sky would be dark and the sunset wasted behind other people's houses. Also, it was impossible to talk in the Spitfire and the things she wanted to say to Hughie could not be shouted.

It didn't matter, anyway. She was not going to Richmond or Chelsea. She was going to work.

She had been planning that stroll over the Albert Bridge since their engagement began. Hughie's proposal should have happened on a walk like that, midstream, between his haunts and hers, but the chance had come and gone before she was ready for it. Albert's was not the only bridge that had to be crossed.

Walking along Battersea Park Road Katy heard urgent footsteps in pursuit and turning round saw Hughie hurrying after her, taking care, as he always did without knowing it, to avoid stepping on cracks in the pavement.

'Aha,' said Hughie. 'A young and beautiful nurse, all alone and without an escort. Can I see you to the door, Miss?'

'Why not?' said Katy, wishing that one day Hughie would just say 'Hullo, darling,' instead of making a speech. Surely he wasn't afraid that someone would overhear him? By now, everyone must know that they were engaged; occasionally she had the uncomfortable feeling that he was trying to conceal the fact, from himself if not from anyone else.

'I think this is the first time I've seen you walking to work,' she said. 'Have you smashed up the Triumph at last?'

'What a dreadful thing to suggest,' said Hughie, pretending shocked amazement. 'Can you really see me wrapped round a lamp post, unwrapped and wheeled into Casualty in three separate bits? You wound me to the heart. No,' he went on, finally remembering to kiss her, 'we are in the midst of an interregnum.'

'A what?'

'It's a Latin word,' said Hughie, pedantically. 'Meaning, between two kings.'

'Oh, we're a king now, are we?'

'Or, in this case, between two cars. Yesterday the Arab

said farewell to his steed —'

'You mean you've sold the Triumph.'

'And tomorrow I take delivery of Doctor Christodoulou's Austin-Healey Sprite, but today, the interregnum.'

'And you're walking,' said Katy, brightly. All she could think was, How much did it cost? How much did it cost?

'Aren't you pleased? If I'd been driving I'd have come the other way and missed you.'

'How much did it cost?'

'Eight hundred, if you must know,' said Hughie, who could see no reason why she should want to know. 'But I got one-fifty for the Spitfire, which eases the pain, somewhat.'

'I thought you wanted a Lotus Elastic.' Thank God he hadn't got one.

'Lotus Elan; or Elite. Of course I want a Lotus Elite. I also want a set of platinum false teeth and Waterford crystal contact lenses. Meanwhile I make do with National Health glasses, amalgam fillings and an Austin-Healey Sprite. Speaking of which, the beast will need some exercise. How about a trip down to Kent on Saturday? Sample the local brews and see the parents.'

'Oh, Hughie, I can't. I'm on nights, aren't I?'

'No chance of time off?'

'Not likely. You know that.' He knew, all right, but she felt that he considered her irregular hours unreasonable, while his were a necessary evil.

'We'll make it the weekend after, then. OK? Or will you be swotting?'

'I should be, but I won't,' said Katy. 'Saturday week, then. I'll look forward to it.' This was not strictly true. She had never met Hughie's family, although it was time she did, and she often wondered what they would make of her as Hughie's fiancée. She had a sudden misgiving.

'You have told them about me, haven't you? I mean – about us?'

'Of course I have,' said Hughie, seeing her doubts and lowering a protective arm about her shoulders. 'Did you think I was ashamed of our awful secret? I can't wait to show you off to them; that's why I suggested *this* Saturday,' he added, virtuously.

Why not last Saturday, then? thought Katy, not entirely reassured. They turned in at the gates of St Angela's. Hughie reclaimed his arm and smiled down at her.

'Have you got time for a coffee before we start?'

'Just about. I've got to go to the common room to fix up about the Bring and Buy on Saturday. I'll see you in the canteen.'

They parted company and Katy headed for the common room to take down one set of notices and put up another. By the time she got back to the canteen Hughie was parked in front of a cup of coffee and had chivalrously provided one for her as well. He was filling in time by chatting with another nurse who got up to leave as Katy approached from behind.

'There goes a nice girl,' said Hughie. 'Who is she?'

'I didn't notice,' said Katy, looking after the departing nurse. 'But she walks like Fleur Barrett.'

'What a very appropriate name,' said Hughie. 'It's French . . .'

'Look,' said Katy, 'I may not have done Latin but I did get O-Level French. It means a flower.'

'Well done. Is she a friend of yours?'

'I don't know her all that well. She's only a second year.'

'A mere babe in arms,' said Hughie. 'Compared with you, that is.'

Katy, although normally persuaded that it was wonderful to be young, was less inclined to think so when Hughie reminded her of her age.

'She must be all of twelve months younger,' said Hughie.

Hughie was twelve years older, nearly thirteen. He was young too, and when she was as old as he was now she would be young still; but by then *he* would be forty-seven.

Better not think about that.

'Hughie?'

'Yes?'

'Did you have to save up for the Sprite?'

'It's nice of you to worry about my poverty,' said Hughie, only half pleasantly. 'No I didn't. I already had the money. I was just waiting for the right car to splash it on.'

'Have you got any left?'

'Good grief!' Hughie banged down his coffee cup. 'What if I have? What if I haven't, come to that? So what? So what? So what?'

Katy stared miserably at the spreading puddle of coffee.

'I didn't mean to cross-question. But shouldn't we be thinking about saving up ourselves?'

'What for?' he said, genuinely perplexed.

'To get married.'

'Good grief,' he said, again. 'Do people still save up to get married? I suppose they do, in certain primitive societies. How quaint.'

'If you mean that Battersea's a primitive society, yes they do,' Katy snapped. 'I'm very primitive myself. I've got a bit in the bank, and some Premium Bonds and – and —'

'And what? Some under the mattress?'

'Never mind.'

'Go on, tell me. Where do you keep it – in your garter?'

'Oh, shut up,' said Katy, swallowing her coffee faster than she liked to and getting up to go. 'Why should you care?'

'You've aroused my curiosity,' said the unrepentant Hughie, beaming. 'You don't hide it in your bra, do you? That's where girls used to keep pound notes at parties when

I was a student. Safest place, I'm told.'

'I dare say it was, in those days,' Katy retorted. 'After all, it was a *very* long time ago. Oh, sit down and finish your drink. It's no good following me. I'm not going to tell you.'

How could she tell him about the yoghurt pots?

The money would have done just as well in the bank, if not better, because it would have been multiplying quietly, but Katy got more pleasure out of having it where she could see it, on the window sill, in a row of family-size yoghurt pots. She had glued down the lids and cut a slit in each, optimistically large enough to take a fifty-pence piece. At the end of the week any loose change went into the yoghurt pots, each of which had a label to show the eventual destination of the money: CHINA; VACUUM CLEANER; CURTAINS; CUTLERY ... It would be nice to get cutlery as a wedding present, but she didn't know anyone who would be able to afford the kind of cutlery that she would like to set before Hughie.

'I think you're barmy,' said her sister Joanne, frankly. 'I bet your Hughie isn't saving up his pennies like this.'

I bet he isn't, thought Katy.

'What's this one for?' Joanne picked up the strawberry yoghurt pot. 'Down payment on a dog kennel? There's not much in it.'

'Linen, can't you read?' said Katy. 'It's not so daft. You'd be surprised how soon it mounts up.'

'What difference'll five p. make? Go on, be a devil; treat yourself to a packet of crisps.'

Katy put the five-pence piece into the linen pot. She wished she had the nerve to start one with BABY on it. There was a spare hazelnut flavour going begging, and it was hard not to think of babies with Rachel, her brother Bernard's wife, expecting another before Christmas.

Rachel was more sympathetic than Joanne had been.

'I used to do that when we were first married, in a pickle jar. It was crazy – I mean, I didn't have tuppence to spare, but I used to enjoy cutting corners just so I could put a bit in my pickle jar. You know, I'd get off the bus one stop early, or smoke two cigarettes less every day until I had the price of a packet, and then I'd put the money in the jar. Bernard said I was pickling it. If I wanted a drink while I was shopping I'd have tea instead of coffee and pickle the difference. I got really fed up, sometimes, but I'd think, it's for the baby. By the time Jason was born that jar was full.'

'What did you buy?'

'Don't laugh,' said Rachel. 'A new exhaust system for the car. The old one dropped off the day he fetched me home from hospital. Oh, don't look so shocked. That kind of thing's not going to happen to you. You're never going to find a doctor short of a few quid in an emergency.'

Katy considered this. Certainly Hughie would never imagine himself going short – because he never had gone short. He wouldn't know how to manage on a shoe-string because he wouldn't recognize a shoe-string if he saw one. How far would his salary stretch once he had someone other than himself to spend it on? He enjoyed seeing her drink the wine and eating the expensive dinners that he bought her, but what sort of a kick would he get out of paying for paraffin and floor polish? Eight hundred pounds for an Austin-Healey Sprite was fine, but what would he say to eighty for a pram? Did he realize that although you got babies for nothing, they began to be expensive immediately afterwards?

The yoghurt pots were a token; a declaration of faith and intent. I AM SAVING UP TO GET MARRIED.

3

There was a certain satisfaction to be had from walking home through the early morning streets when everyone else was going to work. The shops were shut and the lads on the building site hadn't yet had time to work up a full head of steam, so that Katy got past them with nothing more than a few whistles instead of a string of improper invitations that echoed up the road behind her.

When she reached home Dad was unloading nets of vegetables from the van and Mum was downstairs in the shop, polishing up Dunns Seedlings for the front row of the window display, arranging them with the pink spot turned invitingly towards the street.

Mum was downstairs. That was the trouble. If Gran needed anything she banged on the floor with her stick, but she knew better than to bang too often. Mum couldn't afford to miss customers while running up and down to Gran all day, and as soon as Katy got in Gran changed to banging on the wall instead. Katy, in the back bedroom, was on the other side of the wall. Gran, who was too deaf to hear half of what was on the telly and two thirds of what was said to her, never missed Katy's foot on the stairs. Katy went up on the tips of her aching toes, but before she was half way Mum shouted after her, 'Give your Gran a hand with her wash, will you? You know what'll happen if she drops the soap.'

Katy froze and waited for the dreaded stick to begin its tattoo, but she was safe for a few minutes yet. Joanne had the radio on at full volume in the kitchen and Gran had her radio at full volume in the living room, only at a different station. It was impossible that anyone could hear anything above all that, but you were never certain with Gran. Katy went into the kitchen, which was also the living room since Gran took over the real living room, and cleared a space on the table where she could put her books. The table was covered with breakfast crockery which couldn't be put in the sink because last night's washing up was still in soak. Kevin's embryonic hi-fi system, not yet operational and never likely to be, with luck, occupied one corner and on the far side, between the corn flakes and the laundry basket, Joanne lingered over her toast and painted her finger nails green in between mouthfuls.

'Where're you sneaking off to?' said Joanne.

'Sssh! I don't want Gran to hear.'

'You'll be lucky. Her and her bionic ear.'

'Look, if she asks, tell her I'm not home yet.'

Joanne tried to look disapproving.

'You asking me to tell a lie?'

'Yes. Jo, I've got so much to do–revising. Look at this lot.'

'Tough.' Joanne scooped up her own books, suddenly in a hurry. 'I got to go. Feed the gerbils, will you, I didn't get time.' Katy looked at the cage on the draining board.

'Isn't it time they were cleaned out?'

'Yes, well, I haven't got time to do that, either.'

'Tell Kev.'

'I'll tell him, but he won't do it. And I warn you, Gran's got a pain.'

'A bad one?'

'Not bad enough for the doctor but bad enough for Nurse. She's waiting to ask you what it is; not that that'll stop her telling you.'

'If it's bad Mum ought to call the doctor. I can't make a diagnosis.'

Joanne thought that words like that were a way of pulling rank.

'You didn't mind telling me I had a stye coming last week.'

'That wasn't diagnosis; it glowed in the dark.'

Joanne had her revenge.

'Gra-an! Katy's home.'

The following morning Katy decided to put her foot down. She had scarcely reached the landing before being summoned to Gran's bedside to determine whether Gran's sudden pain was wind or a heart attack. Gran was clearly hoping for a heart attack, just a small one to liven things up a bit, and was not at all pleased to be fobbed off with Milk of Magnesia. Katy closed the door on her complaints and prepared for an argument.

Mum called up from the foot of the stairs, 'Are you going shopping this morning?'

'I'm going to bed,' said Katy.

'You always go shopping on Saturdays when you're home.'

'I've just come off nights.' Katy leaned down the stair well. 'I'm going to study for an hour – *in bed* – and then I'm going to sleep.'

'I want you to pick up my coat from the cleaners.'

'Can't Kev or Joanne do that? Mum!' Katy heard her mother's footsteps retreating into the storeroom behind the shop. 'I've got to go back to the hospital this afternoon. I can't stay up all day.'

'What you want to do that for? I don't know why you don't move in there. You treat this place like a hotel.' Mrs Betts raised her voice rather than walk back to the foot of the stairs. Interested customers paused to listen. Gran hammered on the wall.

'If this is a hotel I don't think much of the service,' Katy yelled back. 'I've got to be at the Bring and Buy this afternoon.'

Kevin joined in from the second landing.

'You're supposed to be at *our* Bring and Buy this afternoon. For the youth club. I left all the stuff on your bed.'

'Well, you can just get it off again. I suppose it's old shoes and tea cosies as usual. I want to be in that bed in five minutes flat.'

'And talking of hotels,' her mother screeched, suddenly reappearing in the shop, 'you haven't paid me for last week yet. It won't kill you to run round to the cleaners.'

'What's that got to do with it?' Katy muttered. 'I'm going to bed, now!'

'Gran's gone ever such a funny colour,' said Joanne, coming out of the living room.

'I don't care if she goes bright green,' said Katy.

'Stop fussing,' said Joanne, lazily. 'They can manage their Bring and Buy without you, can't they?'

'I organized it, didn't I? I can't just not turn up. Oh, Gran, what have you done now?'

Joanne lounged in the doorway.

'You should have had more sense than arrange it for when you're on nights.'

'Try and sit up a bit, Gran. I didn't know I was going to be on nights, did I? Can you give us a hand, Jo?' But Joanne had sensibly vanished away like the early morning dew.

'Put the telly on,' said Gran, reviving suddenly as she caught sight of Katy's watch. 'I'm missing *Sesame Street.*'

Katy set her bedside clock for one-thirty, but she forgot to pull out the alarm button, so it was almost three o'clock when she woke. The flat should have been empty except for Gran, who was watching *World of Sport*, and Dad, stewing over his VAT with the pocket calculator that he didn't trust to add up right, but when she went into the kitchen she found Rachel, five months pregnant and looking eight, sitting on the largest chair with Jason balanced on the remains of her lap at the far end of her knee. On the other side of the table, guarding the teapot like a surly bulldog, sat Rachel's mother, Mrs Lake.

Rachel looked round. 'Hullo, Katy. I thought you'd gone out.'

'I should have,' said Katy, searching in vain for someone to blame for her late awakening. 'I'm supposed to be at the hospital.'

'We said we'd go to the Bring and Buy at the youth club,' said Rachel. 'But I couldn't face it. Stop kicking, Jass. I thought you'd be there.'

'So did everyone else,' said Katy. 'Is there any tea left in that pot?'

'Can you take Jason for a minute,' said Rachel. 'If I don't move I'll set.'

'No there isn't,' said Mrs Lake, peering like a fortune teller into the dark interior. She didn't offer to make some more. Katy, wondering if a trek to the hospital was really worth the effort, sat down and took Jason, who dangled sulkily as he was transferred from one lap to the other.

'Don't you want to come to Auntie?'

'Sweetie,' said Jason, addressing nobody in particular. 'Biscuit, 'nana, ice cream, Mars Bar,' he went on, knowing that sooner or later he would get something, if only to shut him up.

'You should help your mother when she asks you,' said Mrs Lake, plugging her grandson with a banana. Katy wondered if it would be any use hinting to Rachel that Jason was horribly overweight, and that if she and Bernard really wanted him to end up the same shape as Grandma Lake, they were going the right way about it.

Better not.

'I can't be in two places at once. There's a Bring and Buy at the hospital as well. I'm supposed to be there, actually.'

'You should put your family first,' said Mrs Lake, managing to suggest that Katy was an undutiful daughter. 'You can choose your friends but you can't choose your family,' she chanted, obscurely.

'I don't want to go to the hospital either,' Katy said defensively. 'I'm on nights this week, in Casualty. My feet are raw.'

'You're young,' said Mrs Lake, as though youth were a criminal act, deserving of sore feet. 'It's Rachel who ought to be resting. Look at her ankles.'

Katy looked.

'Have you told your doctor about that?'

'No need,' said Rachel. 'I'm all right if I put my feet up.'

'You ought to, anyway.'

'What is it then, *Nurse Betts*?' demanded Mrs Lake, daring her to tell them. 'I suppose you've got some long name for it. It looks like swollen ankles to me.'

'Yes, but —'

'But nothing. You're still a trainee, aren't you?'

'Student.'

'I've had five. Allow me to know something about it. All of them forceps except Rachel, and she —'

'I'd better get along to the sale,' said Katy, gently pushing Jason to the floor and scraping banana pulp from her skirt. 'Go to Grandma, love. Auntie's got to go out.'

Jason reeled across the kitchen, poked the remains of his banana into the gerbils' cage and began whanging the canary's bars with the skin. As Katy went into the bedroom she heard Mrs Lake's voice, rising with resentment.

'That's nurses all over. You can't tell them *any*thing.'

The sale room was pleasantly empty when she arrived. The professionals, always the first in the queue, had picked the clothing stall clean, leaving only the garments that would never fit anyone but the people they were made for; size wxx with arms so long that they had gravel rash on their knuckles. The food counter was empty and the only activity was round the White Elephant stall which was always good for a laugh if you didn't happen to be trying to sell what was on it. Anna Newcross was drinking tea behind the gift stall and half-heartedly rearranging the items that no one would buy because they could be got cheaper in Boots.

'Oh, you didn't get hit by a bus, then,' said Anna. 'We'd given you up.'

'I overlaid. Sorry. Look, I'll buy something to make up,' said Katy. 'Come on, sell me a bargain.'

'They aren't bargains,' said Anna. 'That's why nobody buys them. How about some Primitive Man?'

'Some what?'

'Primitive Man. It's after-shave. Haven't you seen it on the Box? In comes Primitive Man himself, dragging a dead dinosaur. "It brings out the beast in you" he says, and hits his lady wife over the head with a club. Very liberated. Get some for Hughie.'

'Don't want to give him ideas. It might work,' said Katy. She took off the cap and sniffed. 'It smells like ether and washing-up liquid.' The bottle was in a box covered in tawny flock paper, with brown liver marks on it.

'Leopard skin,' said Anna. 'I'll knock off five p. seeing as it's for a friend.'

Katy moved to the other end of the stall and checked over the usual silt of oven gloves, hostess aprons and egg cosies knitted to look like little men with pointed heads. Pinned to the front of the table were three tea towels. Katy stooped down to look at them. They were just the kind of tea towel she would want hanging in her kitchen, when she had a kitchen to hang them in; and not on a hook, either, but draped over one of those stainless steel racks that had arms sticking out of the wall, so that everyone could see the pattern.

One was white with a wreath of yellow and brown daisies on it, one was dark blue with a green and gold sea-horse, coiling his tail round a frond of seaweed. The third was red, with a single white rose in the middle. They were so bright and fresh they made even the end-of-sale detritus look cheerful, and how they would shine in her beautiful kitchen, where old mother Lake would never once set her horrible flat feet and Jason would be banned until Rachel had house-trained him. They still had knife-edged creases where they had been folded and packed before someone opened them out and pinned them up like flags. Katy un-pinned them and took them to Anna.

'How much are these?' Damn the price; she was going to have them.

'Oh, they're reduced,' said a woman, leaning over from the next stall. 'No one will buy them. I told 'em, they're useless for drying until they've been washed a dozen times. You have to boil 'em and boil 'em.'

'Well! No wonder no one would buy them,' said Anna, exasperated. 'Are you sure you want them, Katy? They're ninety pence each.'

'That's reduced?'

'They'd be over a pound in the shops. They're linen.'

'They should dry up all right, then.'

'They're cotton,' said the woman who favoured boiling.

'It says linen here on the bottom. I'll take them.' For crying out loud: two pounds seventy for three tea towels. What did a table-cloth cost? She would have to make do with those straw place mats from the Oxfam shop.

4

Katy went along to the florist's in the precinct and bought a bunch of flowers. She wanted roses but you got more daisies for the same money.

'They aren't daisies,' said the assistant, wrapping them, and told Katy a long name that left her none the wiser. She thought of them as daisies because they reminded her of the tea towel from the Bring and Buy. They matched her newly finished dress, too, and she couldn't resist turning back the wrapping paper so that all the flowerless people in the street could admire the daisies and the dress together as she walked to Hughie's flat.

They were going to drive down to Kent to visit Hughie's parents. Without knowing it, Katy wanted all the admiration she could command, right now, in case she didn't get any later on. By the time she arrived at the flat the daisies looked tawdry, the dress garish; she was convinced that the day was going to turn out a total disaster.

'You're early,' said Hughie, letting her in. She had a key of her own so she guessed that he had been watching out for her, which restored her confidence a little until she caught sight of the fierce photograph of the parents that Hughie kept on his desk. They peered at her from the lawn of their green Kentish garden: there's that greengrocer's daughter from Battersea, they hissed to each other, without turning their heads.

'Look, Hughie, what do you call them? What do *I* call them?'

Hughie looked thrown for once.

'Well, I can't keep calling them Mr and Mrs Evans, can I? I mean, not once I know them.'

'Oh, I see. You don't really need to call them anything, do you?' said Hughie. 'It's only in radio plays that people address each other by name, so that you know who's talking. Hullo, Mothah! Hullo, Fathah!'

'Is that what you call them?'

'No, it isn't. Just Dad and, er, Mummy, actually.'

'Mummy!' Katy let this sink in.

'Why not? Let's get going, then. Didn't you bring a coat?'

'What for?'

'You'll be chilly in the car with the roof down.'

'I've got my shawl.'

'I think you'll need a coat.'

'Why, to hide the dress? Isn't this good enough for Mothah and Fathah?'

'Don't be silly,' said Hughie. 'You look lovely.' He was very put out. Katy thought he was right to be put out, but on the other hand she thought he ought to guess how wretchedly nervous she was feeling. Five minutes ago she would have agreed that the dress looked lovely, now she wasn't so sure and looked over her shoulder at the mirror.

'Are you afraid they'll think you've hitched yourself to someone common?'

'Katy, don't do yourself down,' he said. 'They won't think anything of the sort, and if they did, to hell with it. Surely it's what I think that's important, and you know what I think.'

'I know,' said Katy, wishing she could make a joke of it. 'But I'm so afraid they won't like me.'

'Of course they'll like you. Why shouldn't they?'

Katy could think of a number of reasons, and followed Hughie down to the car very slowly, taking care not to catch her heels on the stairs. Suppose they were the kind of people who made snap decisions; who sized you up as soon as they saw you? If they were like that she knew that it was no more than she deserved, because she was just like that herself. She had made up her mind about *them* from a photograph.

Hughie's new Sprite was drawn up to the kerb in the street behind his flat. Katy climbed down into it and pushed the daisies behind the seat where she could forget them, determined to enjoy as much of the journey as she could without thinking about what lay at the end of it.

The car was small and rolled along very close to the ground, but once they were out of London and on the M2, Hughie began to get larger ideas.

'Ever see a Hispano-Suiza?' he yelled, above the roar of the tyres and the slipstream.

'Is that an operation or an apparatus?' said Katy, half joking but wondering if it were something she ought to know about. Question papers swam before her eyes.

Which of the following is diagnosed by the Guthrie blood test?

Phenylketonurea.

Galactosaemia.

Hispano-Suiza.

'It was a car, you ignorant female,' said Hughie, lifting his hands from the wheel in a gesture of despair. 'The most beautiful —'

The rest of his hymn of praise was drowned by an over-taking artic. Katy sank down in her seat as far as the belt would allow. How would she ever keep up with him? Every time he opened his mouth he came out with a re-mark that she didn't understand. What if the rest of the family were like that? She imagined them all standing around on their green Kentish lawn with elegant glasses in their hands, braying incomprehensible comments to each other in high, self-satisfied voices, like top people in adverts on the telly. No wonder Hughie had looked so stunned when she took him home to the flat above the shop. He must have wondered what he had let himself in for, just as she was wondering now. She looked sideways at him as he swung the car from lane to lane in pursuit of the artic that had dared to outrun him. He was always protective towards her when they went out together; unfortunately, he didn't seem to know what she needed protection from.

He saw her looking and thought that he had scared her with his reckless driving. The protective look reappeared on his face and he slowed down. That much he could understand.

They turned off the motorway at the Faversham slip road and drove back among the trees that they had looked down on earlier. Katy felt less at ease now that she was looking up at them. On the motorway they had seldom been out of sight of the oil refineries and power stations of the estuary. Now, suddenly, there was not a building anywhere. The trees hung over the road on one side and on the other, fields rose steeply to a bald horizon where the crops had been shaved away. Katy was used to a view that appeared in slices between buildings. This view was unavoidable. They were in it.

'Where are we?'

'God knows,' said Hughie, cheerfully. 'I only know the road.'

'But didn't you used to live here?'

'*I* never did. I told you, we were always on the move when I were a lad.' His voice became a village idiot's rustic burr. 'Oi be a furriner in these 'ere parrrrts.'

'Would you want to live in a place like this?' Katy persisted. The fields grew steeper. They were turning into hills.

'Not on your life. I can't wait to get back to civilization after a week in the wilds.'

'That's good,' said Katy. 'Because I wouldn't, either.'

'Oh?' Hughie seemed surprised that she should have given the matter any thought.

'Where shall we live, do you think?'

'Dreaming of roses round the door?'

'Not on your life. Central heating,' said Katy.

In spite of the fact that he described his parents' house as dead ordinary and quite small, Katy guessed that his ideas of small and ordinary might not be the same as hers. Clearly it would be larger than the greengrocery, and the more she thought about it the larger it became, until she was picturing a minor mansion, set in grounds only less extensive than Battersea Park. Occasionally chimneys showed above the trees, or double gates opened on to a winding drive, but she knew better than to ask, 'Is this it?'

At last they drove into a village. The street was narrow and the houses leaned on each other along one side. The mansion immediately shrunk to a kind of Snow White's cottage with hollyhocks and thatch, like the ones on Gran's antimacassars. Across the road the parish church squatted in a bosky graveyard; rose bushes lined the walk from the lich-gate to the porch. Katy imagined herself coming down that walk, between the roses.

'Hughie, is that your parents' church?'

'I dare say it would be if they went to church. We're almost there. They probably drop in at Christmas and nod to God.'

'It'd be a nice place to get married. Wouldn't it?'

'A step up from St Asaph's, Lavender Hill, certainly.

With your family holding up an arcade of cucumbers over the path,' said Hughie. He turned left, away from the village, and on the next corner stood a brown brick house; not at all small, but dead ordinary; also dead square, with a window at each corner and a door in the middle, like a child's drawing of a house. A cowed privet hedge slunk round the side of the garden which was divided neatly in two by a woven fence; vegetables at the back, flower beds and the green Kentish lawn at the front, a patch of frazzled grass with a manhole cover in the middle. In the rear a plantation of fir trees slithered downhill towards it. Katy was not so much relieved by its plainness as disappointed. It was hardly worth all her misgivings but nevertheless, the parents were in there.

'Is this it?'

'Yes. Out you get.'

Katy turned cold.

'Hughie, I'm nervous.'

'No you're not,' said Hughie, heartily, but he looked at her at last and saw that she was. 'I'll look after you,' he said. 'Don't worry.'

Unable to explain quite how she felt, Katy knew that she did not precisely want to be looked after. Slowly she unfastened the seat belt and got out of the car, while Hughie bounced out on his side and slammed the door.

'Aren't you going to lock it?'

'We aren't in the heart of London's gangland now, you know,' he said, opening the gate. 'Come on.'

'Hughie ...'

'Come *on*. They're quite harmless. Anyway, we shan't be seeing them again for ages so it doesn't really matter if you don't get on.'

'It matters to me,' said Katy.

Hughie took her hand and kissed her, right there in the

gateway, under the wall-eyed gaze of his parents' house. Reassured, she let him lead her into the garden.

'Time and the hour run through the roughest day,' said Hughie as they went up the long straight path. 'That's *Macbeth.* Shakespeare,' he added, helpfully.

'I read it at school,' said Katy. 'They had his head off by the end of that day.'

The path was horribly exposed, with nothing but flat lawn on either side. The nearest thing you could hide behind was a seedy bush which had suffered from being clipped into the shape of a coffee percolator.

'That's Dad's topiary,' said Hughie. 'It's supposed to be a peacock. Don't admire it just to be polite – he knows it's a disaster.'

'All right.' The house stared and Katy stared back, imagining Hughie's mother on hands and knees in her living room, eyes level with the window sill to observe them as they approached the front door. The front door opened and there was Hughie's mother, looking nothing at all like Hughie and wearing the kind of clothes that Royalty likes when off-duty. Katy immediately felt over-dressed, as though she had turned up at a disco in a ball gown.

'Hullo, darlings.' She kissed Hughie. 'This must be Polly.'

'This is Katy,' said Hughie, winking over the top of his mother's head.

Katy took off her shawl with much flashing of the engagement ring, so that Mrs Evans should be in no doubt about her status, and wondering if 'Polly' was a mere slip of the tongue, or whether Mrs Evans had been expecting a different fiancée.

'Let's have some tea. Tea, Katy?'

'I thought something a little stronger?' Hughie suggested.

'Daddy will be back with a bottle or two directly,' said

his mother. 'I expect Katy would like some tea, anyway.'

'Tea's fine, thanks,' said Katy, and followed Mrs Evans into the living room, over the springy carpet. The house was nicely furnished; not the kind of things she would want for herself, but nice. Looking down to see the pattern on the carpet she noticed that Hughie's mother had really appalling varicose veins and realized that if she steered the conversation carefully, they would not be short of something to talk about. There need be no awkward pauses while each tried to think of something to say to the other. Once Mrs Evans understood that she was a nurse – and Katy was not convinced that Mrs Evans knew anything about her yet – there would be no holding her back.

She was right.

By the time they left, she could have written a five-star case history on Mrs Evans, beginning with the veins and working upwards, organ by organ until they reached the neck, where Mrs Evans cherished an unidentified swelling. Hughie and his father retired to the kitchen to be away from the clinical chit-chat, and when it was time to go, Mrs Evans said good-bye to Katy with real animation. She, at least, had had a lovely day. She ought to get on well with Gran.

'Who's a clever girl, then?' said Hughie, as they drove home in twilight.

'Search me,' said Katy. 'Polly? Who's Polly?'

'Polly?'

'Your mother said "Hullo Polly" when she saw me. Was she your last?'

'My brother's last but ten, I should imagine,' said Hughie. 'He's a fast worker. I'm going to keep him away from you.'

She had to be content with that. It sounded reasonable.

'Well, who *is* this clever girl then?'

'You are,' he said. 'My mother thinks you're wonderfully sympathetic. That's what she said, while you were in the loo.'

'She talked and I listened.'

'That's what I mean,' said Hughie. 'That's just what she wanted. They haven't lived there long and she hasn't any friends in the village. You've got nothing to worry about, there.'

'What about your dad?'

'He agrees with me – thinks you are too beyewtiful to be true,' said Hughie, embarrassed at repeating even a second-hand compliment. 'Look, it's going to rain. I'd better stop and put the hood up.'

While he was doing it, Katy discovered the daisies, still jammed behind the seat. She quietly tipped them out of the door while he was busy on the other side of the car. She had managed very well without them.

'Do we have to go back on the motorway?' she said, as he lowered himself into the car and the first drops of rain began to spit against the taut covering of the hood.

'No, but it's easier.'

'Never mind being easier,' said Katy. 'It's nice in here, with all that weather outside, and the trees blowing about. I like being so low down. It feels safe.'

'If one of those trees comes down on top of us it won't feel so safe,' said Hughie. 'This is the end of summer, by the look of it.'

'About time,' said Katy. 'The schools went back last week. Well, can we go home the long way?'

'Anything for you,' said Hughie. This was not his usual philosophy. 'As it happens, there's a Free House just before we get to Sittingbourne. We could stop and have supper there, and a few jars of the real thing, and then back to my place. You are staying tonight, aren't you?' he said, anxiously.

'Yes,' said Katy. 'Wouldn't it be nice if I could always stay, every night? I think about it all the time, Hughie.'

But he had nothing to add to that.

5

Elaine sat at her dressing table, making herself beautiful for the company director who was supposed to be taking her Up West for the evening. Katy had met the company director and was of the opinion that Elaine could spare herself the trouble since his attention was mainly taken up with his own appearance. He walked along streets with his eyes turned sideways, ready to catch his reflection in shop windows.

'Tell you what,' said Elaine, 'you could be a bridesmaid.'

'At your wedding? That'd be the third time. First when Bernard got married, then my cousin Marina. Now you. No thanks. You can be matron of honour at mine.'

'One fine day,' said Elaine. 'Third time lucky,' she said, brightly, taking it for granted that Katy was getting desperate, since she would have been. She took a paper pattern out of the drawer and tossed it across the bed. 'Look, this is my dress – see? Quilted sleeves and looped up at the front with a quilted underskirt, and satin-stitch embroidery on the bodice. If you were a bridesmaid this one would be yours. A sort of apple green, I thought. It'd suit you. You'd look nice standing next to my sister; you're about her height.'

'Who's making them?' said Katy, looking at the patterns and deciding, there and then, that under no circumstances was she going to be Elaine's bridesmaid in that miserable little tube of a dress with a frill round the bottom, designed, like all bridesmaids' dresses, to make the wearer appear so stout and plain that the bride couldn't help but look radiant.

'My aunt's making mine. I'm not having a veil, though. It looks so daft if there's a bit of wind. I'm getting one of those big cartwheel hats instead, with long ribbons – you'd make your own dress, wouldn't you? You're good at that.'

'Hats blow off, too,' said Katy.

'Yeah, but they don't stand on end.'

'What about a going-away dress?'

'I'll think about that later. I don't know that we are going away, yet. Chris isn't the honeymoon sort.' Chris was the company director. Elaine looked every which way but at Katy. 'Chris's old man said he'd pay for the honeymoon or we could put the money towards a flat. It'll probably be the flat.'

'Haven't you got anywhere to live, yet?'

'Plenty of time for that,' said Elaine, quickly.

'But it's less than two months. You don't want to end up here living with your mum.'

'Fat chance. She's only just got rid of my sister and *her* family.'

'Or apart.'

'Aren't you cheerful?' said Elaine, pouting. 'You really love life, don't you?'

'It's the first thing I'd think of. Suppose you have kids.'

'Of course we'll have kids. No point in getting married otherwise, is there?'

'I thought you didn't like babies.'

'I don't like other people's babies,' said Elaine, firmly. 'Do you know where *you're* going to live yet?'

Katy had walked into this trap and had to flounder out of it as best she could.

'Hughie won't have any trouble getting a mortgage,' she said, resolving to mention it this evening, as soon as she arrived at his flat.

'Your loony doctor? When am I going to meet him, or don't they let him out in the daytime? I suppose the trouble is getting him to get a mortgage.'

Katy was saved by Mrs Bryant, who put her head round the door and said, 'Christopher's here.'

The company director was in the hall, adjusting his tie, polishing his hair and looking at his watch.

'I guess I'll get here one day and find you ready,' he said, addressing not Elaine but her reflection in the mirror. Elaine came over all meek and went to fetch her coat.

The company director turned up his eyes to the ceiling.

'Women!' he said to Katy, as though Katy hardly counted as one and could be safely asked for an unbiased opinion. 'Is that your uniform? Don't you ever wear civvies?'

'I've just come off duty, as it happens.'

'Why do they make you wear those hideous raincoats? You look like a schoolgirl. I thought nurses wore cloaks with sexy red satin lining.'

'Not in the street. Excuse me.' Katy edged round him. 'I can't hang about.'

'Pity,' said the company director, rotating on his pointed toes to keep her in view. 'A pity. I expect we'll meet again.'

'I expect so. Good-bye,' said Katy, in a hurry to be gone before Elaine came back, grovelling.

'You wouldn't have any trouble getting a mortgage, would you?' said Katy.

'You know what "mortgage" means, don't you?' said Hughie. 'Dead pledge. What a thought. Eat drink and be merry, for tomorrow we have a mortgage.'

'How else are we to get a place, then?' said Katy. 'You weren't thinking of buying a caravan and hitching it up behind the Sprite? I mean, we are going to live together after we're married, aren't we, or did you have other plans? Me and the kids in a hostel and you on Waterloo Station.'

'Kids? What kids? I see no kids,' said Hughie, looking round.

'Not yet; but eventually. I want children, you know that.'

'So what's the hurry? We're too young.'

'Well, you won't exactly be wasting your youth, will you?' said Katy, unkindly. 'You've already had it.'

'You don't want to get tied down,' said Hughie, easily, as if he were reading his answers off an optician's chart. 'You don't want to waste all your training.'

'Elaine wants kids and she doesn't even like them.'

'Who's Elaine? She sounds like an evil influence. Women shouldn't get together in corners and talk. They get ideas.'

'She's a friend of mine who's getting married. I expect we'll get an invitation to the wedding.' Could she accept? What on earth would Hughie and Elaine find to say to each other? 'She wanted me to be her bridesmaid if I didn't get married first, only I don't know if I'll get time off, so I had to say no – oh. Don't worry,' said Katy, seeing Hughie's expression. 'I'm not in a hurry. I know there's plenty of time. I just don't want to waste that time. I mean, I'm saving. I'd start buying things, sheets and crockery and that, if I knew I was going to have somewhere to put them.' She thought of the three tea towels at the top of the wardrobe.

'What are we doing tonight?' said Hughie, changing the subject abruptly, as he ran out of arguments.

'The usual, I suppose,' said Katy. 'It doesn't look as though we've got anything to talk about. What *are* we going to talk about in the evenings, Hughie? Compression ratios? Real ale? How to make your own saxophone out of milk bottle tops?'

The phone rang. Hughie answered it, his replies of 'Yes. Yes. Yes', becoming increasingly resigned. Before he had put down the receiver his free hand was reaching behind him, for his coat.

'If we have any evenings,' said Katy.

Hughie was half out of the door. 'You can talk. Last time we had a free evening you stayed at home with a cosy case history.'

'It won't always be like that.'

'I should hope not. What are you going to do now? Run home and swot?'

'I'll wait here.'

'And swot.'

'Yes, but I will be waiting.'

'I don't know how long I'll be.'

'I'll still wait.'

'Bless you.' He came back and kissed her. 'Something warm to come home to.'

I wish he wouldn't say things like that, thought Katy, hearing him run downstairs. Something warm to come home to – he makes me sound like a cup of cocoa. It puts my teeth on edge already when he says things like that; what will it be like after I've listened to him for ten years – or twenty – or —

Oh Gawd! I could be married for fifty years, like Gran was.

It was very dark when he came back, dark enough to risk saying something silly without being seen.

'Hughie; did I tell you about my yoghurt pots?'

'What a moment to start talking about yoghurt. You've no poetry in you, woman.'

'Not yoghurt. The pots. I've got this row of them on the window sill – I put all my loose change in them – saving up.'

Hughie said nothing.

'You can laugh if you like. Everyone else does.'

'I'm not laughing.'

'It's just that it makes me feel I'm getting somewhere. When I go past shops I keep thinking, I'd like that in the lounge. That'd be nice in the bedroom. I want to start getting things together.' The tea towels flew like flags in the darkness.

Silence.

'Don't you?'

'There's no hurry.'

'I know, but the whole point of an engagement is to give yourself time to get ready. So that when you get married, everything *is* ready.'

'Ah, the nesting instinct,' said Hughie. 'You'll get over it.'

I don't want to get over it.

'Is that your professional opinion?' said Katy, sitting up. 'Are you going to suggest treatment? Aversion therapy?'

'Oh, stop worrying and come back here.'

'I'm going home,' said Katy.

'To count your yoghurt pots?'

Joanne quarrelled with her boy friend once a week and tonight was the night. She lay on her bed and consoled herself with an uplifting magazine story about a lady who had had six major operations but still ran a market garden and won ballroom dancing competitions. From time to time she consulted Katy for professional advice about the operations.

'Katy, what's a peptic ulcer?'

'Katy, what's a pulmonary embolism?'

'Katy, what's haemoglobin?'

Katy lay on the other bed surrounded by medical literature of a less entertaining nature.

'If you're so interested,' she said at last, 'you can help me with my revision.'

'I don't know about that,' said Joanne, looking round for an escape. 'You ought to ask Kev. He's better with all those long words.'

'You've been doing all right up to now,' said Katy. 'Come on, be nice for once. Just help us out, won't you?' she tossed a book across the room and it landed on Joanne's stomach.

'What you want me to do?'

'Just go through and pick a question.'

'Which one?'

'Any one. That's the point. I could get asked anything in my finals. I've got to be *ready* for anything.'

Joanne skipped through the pages.

'What about endocrinology?'

'Fine. Go on.'

'I dunno. Look at this – toxic nodular goitre. I don't like the sound of that. Let's have something else ... What are hormones?'

Katy told her.

'Don't go so fast,' Joanne complained. 'I can't keep up.'

'Well, was I right?'

'I don't know. I couldn't understand half the words. They don't sound like they look. Let's find something easy.'

'I don't want something easy.'

'Easy for me, I mean. Nice short little English words. Ah, here we are. What do you do if the patient falls out of bed?'

'Does it say —'

'Hey!' Joanne sat upright. 'What can the nurse learn from inspecting vomit? That's sick, isn't it?'

'Let's get the patient back into bed, first.'

'You have to inspect sick? I mean, look at it?'

'Yes,' said Katy irritably. 'And that's not all we have to inspect.'

Joanne threw the book at her. 'How dis*gust*ing. You test yourself, mate. I'm not reading any more of that.'

Elaine picked up the book by one corner.

'You're joking. You don't really expect me to . . .'

'I don't expect anybody to do anything,' said Katy. 'D'you mind if I just sit here and look at it? It's so noisy at home. But it would help if you'd sort of pick out a question and let me answer it.'

'You pick out your own questions,' said Elaine. 'There's words in there a nice girl shouldn't know. What would Christopher say?'

'He probably doesn't know them either,' said Katy. Elaine kept quiet for a while, trying to work out whether or not the company director had sustained a severe insult.

'I've got a multi-choice paper here,' said Katy, hopefully. 'There's nothing nasty on that.'

'No way,' said Elaine. 'Put 'em all back in the bag and let's talk about something cheerful. Doesn't it turn you up, sometimes?'

'Being cheerful?'

'Nursing. I mean, doesn't it make you sick – really sick?'

'Not any more,' said Katy. 'When I first started, everything turned me up. I mean, I felt ill half the time – I didn't want to eat when I got home, but not any more. Tell you what, though – I still don't like handling sputum.'

'What's sputum?'

'Are you sure you want to know?' said Katy, grinning.

'Probably not. Look, I'll show you my hat for the wedding. You are coming, aren't you?'

'I'll try, I told you. It's a big one, isn't it? Let's hope it isn't windy.'

'I'll have it pinned on. What about when you get people brought in all smashed up and with their insides hanging out, and that?'

'If you looked at the book you'd see that there's procedures for all that. You don't have time to feel ill. You just follow the procedure.'

'Just like that?'

'There's things that have to be done, and you do them.'

'Funny,' said Elaine. 'I never thought of you as efficient. You didn't used to be.' A thought seemed to strike her for the first time. 'Are you a good nurse?'

'Yes,' said Katy, without hesitating. Elaine raised her eyebrows. 'Does that sound conceited? It isn't, really. If I knew I wasn't a good nurse I'd have packed it in by now. I know what's got to be done and I do it. That's what we're there for.'

'You sound like an army recruiting poster,' said Elaine. 'Join the Professionals. Don't you ever get in a panic?'

'No ... not any more.'

'Go on,' said Elaine.

'I told you: no.'

'You were going to say something else. I could tell,' said Elaine. 'Something happened, did it?'

'No.'

'You made a mess-up of something? Somebody died? Is it a secret?' Elaine sounded curious, but sympathetic.

'It's a sort of secret – I mean, I never told anybody. Nothing much.'

'You can tell me, can't you?' said Elaine. 'I don't go tattling. Anyway,' she added, frankly, 'I like hospital gossip.'

'Hospital gossip is sex, mostly,' said Katy. 'This wasn't in the hospital; that was the trouble. I mean, like when you said I was efficient. It's easy to be efficient on the ward. You know your way about. The patients expect you to know your way about. *They* don't. You've got your cap and apron on and you're always there. They're frightened, and they see the uniform and they know that Nurse is in charge. And it's catching. You do the right things because they expect you to do them. They're ill and in bed – you're walking about. It's easy.'

'Yer,' said Elaine, wondering what was coming. 'So what went wrong?'

'Nothing went wrong. I was round at Hughie's one night. We were going out – I was all dressed up – and I had to go back to the hospital. There'd been an explosion in a restaurant.'

'A bomb?' Elaine began to look really interested.

'No; it was a gas main, I think. An accident. Anyway, they brought the casualties to St Angela's, but some of us got sent out there; there were people trapped. I wasn't expecting anything like that. I didn't have my uniform or anything. I wasn't feeling like a nurse; I wasn't ready.'

'And you should have been?'

'Of course I should have been – anyway, that wasn't the point. They gave us special clothing, and helmets, because they thought the place would collapse, and I got sent in with this woman who'd got trapped. A beam had come down across her legs. Her husband was dead.'

'Did you have to tell her?'

'I think she knew. Anyway, you get used to that. I didn't have to do anything but stay with her while they tried to get her out. The firemen were trying to lift the beam away, but they couldn't get it up far enough, and the walls were caving in. Every time they moved it rubble came down all over us. I kept thinking I could see the walls moving. I don't suppose they were, but when I look back I can sort of see the cracks between the bricks getting wider and then closing again. And *she* could see them too. She was screaming to be let out, and she couldn't move. *And I couldn't do anything.* I couldn't give her anything; the doctor wouldn't allow it. I just had to sit there and hold her and say, "They're getting you out. They're getting you out. It's all right. It's all right." And she said, "It's all right for you." She thought it was my fault for not doing anything. She had to scream at me, there wasn't anybody else. You see, like, she thought it was easy for me to talk. She thought I didn't understand how it felt – but I *did*. For the first time, I understood, and I couldn't help her.'

'So it wasn't your fault.' Elaine was evidently beginning to wish that she hadn't invited Katy to confide in her. Blood and guts was one thing, but an uneasy conscience was too much to handle.

'Nothing was anybody's fault. But they couldn't move the beam. The doctor said they would have to amputate to get her out.'

'What! Cut off her leg?'

'Below the knee. They didn't tell her, but she knew something was going to happen. She screamed and cried, and I cried.'

'I'm not surprised,' said Elaine, but Katy could see that she was.

'I cried because I was frightened. I couldn't do any of the things I'd been trained to do and I was on my own. I couldn't call Sister. I didn't *know* what to do. See, you can go through that book, and those papers, and you won't find anything like that.'

6

'How's Hughie these days?' said Anna, crossing the corridor in the opposite direction. 'I haven't seen him lately.'

Nor had Katy. 'Tell you what,' she said, 'if I'd given away a quid to everyone who's asked me how Hughie is today, I'd be skint.'

Anna looked slightly taken aback. 'Well, we all like to know how our hospital romances are going on.'

'Do we? You make it sound like one of these books Jay's always reading. She had one the other day; *Doctor Ballantyne's Secret*. You know what the secret was? He was having it off with Sister Casualty. I looked at the end.'

'That's cheating.'

'You don't think I was going to wade through all that rubbish just to find out what happened, do you? I mean, no chance it wouldn't have a happy ending,' said Katy, not at all pleased to hear her engagement described as a hospital romance.

'All romances have a happy ending,' said Anna, and left Katy to make what she could of this last remark. Anna was a fine one to talk about happy endings.

Since she was now off-duty she took out her engagement ring and slid it on to her finger before going into the canteen. Then she stopped by the door and stared at it. Even after all this time she was surprised to see it there; perhaps because she wore it so little it still felt strange. It tended to work round so that the stone dug into the next finger and this slight discomfort remained a discomfort instead of a reassuring reminder that someone had asked her to marry him. Elaine's ring had worn a groove in *her* finger, but it turned out that there had been two other rings there previously, preparing the ground. Elaine admitted to having sold one and returned the other, but that was all she would say. What did you do with a redundant engagement ring? And what a horrible thought to be having. For some reason Katy saw tea towels.

She took her cup to a table where the only occupant was reading a book and seemed unlikely to break off to ask her how Hughie was. Unfortunately she closed the book almost as soon as Katy sat down. It was Helen Hammond, an SEN who tended to treat comparative strangers as dear old friends and accordingly felt free to ask them impertinent questions. Katy saw very little of her and, on the whole, was glad of it.

Helen, familiar as she might be, was no good at names.

'Hello, Kath.'

'Hi,' said Katy, wishing that she had a book of her own to disappear behind. Whipping out a knitting pattern wouldn't look very convincing.

'How's Hughie?'

Katy ground her teeth.

'He's all right.'

'He was all right last night, wasn't he? Where were you?'

'Come again?'

'At the disco over The Rising Sun. It was him, wasn't it? I mean, I assumed it was, but I didn't see you, so I did wonder.'

Katy looked at Helen's beaming, vindictive dial and longed to pour the tea over her head, wondering frantically; does she know I wasn't there? Is she sure or is she trying to find out? Hughie never went to a disco in his life if he could help it. He can't have gone to one without me.

In a prim and overly responsible voice she said, 'I've got

my finals next month. I don't go out just when I feel like it. Still, I can't expect him to stay at home just because I do.'

'You knew where he was, then?' Helen probed like a surgeon after an unidentified foreign object.

'No, I didn't, actually,' said Katy. 'He doesn't have to ask my permission to go out. And I don't have to ask his. We don't live in each other's pockets. So long as we trust each other we can go where we like and no harm done; and you can't come to much harm at The Rising Sun.' The useful, ready-made phrases came out pat, as though she had them packaged and waiting. Helen continued to smile blandly.

'Have I said something I shouldn't?'

'You can say what you like,' said Katy. 'I've never met anyone who listens.'

She got up and walked out of the canteen, leaving her tea untouched, and feeling the smile between her shoulders, all the way to the door.

If only she knew where to find Hughie she would go up and accost him and demand to know what the hell he was playing at. He knew perfectly well that she had stayed at home to study last night. He should also know, perfectly well, how much she hated doing it. Did he really imagine that she was using her exams as an excuse not to see him? Did he really believe, in that case, that she preferred sitting in her shared and undersized bedroom, hands over ears to shut out the canary, the hi-fi, the radio, the two televisions and Dad's jig-saw, desperately trying to commit a case study to memory; preferred that misery to being with him?

If he did think that, then he was the loony Elaine said he was.

She was horribly upset, and also slightly shocked to discover that it hadn't really come as a surprise.

On the way out of the building she paused by the notice board to take down an out-of-date announcement for a river trip to Hampton Court. It had been the last outing of the summer and she had looked forward to it, thinking that it would be her final fling before she settled down to work for her exams; an end to the seemingly endless programme of functions and outings, darts matches and discos that she had arranged during the year. Hampton Court would have been her farewell appearance; Hampton Court, Hughie and herself, all in one lovely day; and then, she hadn't been able to go.

She had assumed that he hadn't gone either, out of sympathy, and he had allowed her to think it, but *had* he gone, without her? Come to think of it, no one had said much about it, afterwards, except to ask her, interminably, how Hughie was.

Hughie, it seemed, was doing very well without her. Katy screwed up the notice and walked on towards the exit thinking hard and silently cursing Helen and her nasty inquiries for making her think. At the back of her mind she was compiling a list of Hughie's shortcomings that she had refused to notice before, and at the head of the list was the inescapable fact that he *could* do without her. She needed him but he didn't need her. Very well, he should have the chance to find out how he felt when he couldn't have her at all. She decided to tell him, at the first opportunity, that she wanted a cooling-off period, like the Unions did. That way he would find out.

And she would find out . . .

All she found out at first was that it made very little difference. For a week she did not go out with Hughie, but before now she had survived ten days, a fortnight even, without seeing him, except on duty. After a while, however, she noticed that there was a difference. She had engineered the situation and she was in control. She was unhappy, but it was her own doing, not his. He took to lurking. She would not be moved.

Towards the end of the afternoon the Casualty department became less congested, as though the prospect of a fine evening were too good to waste in being ill. There were only five or six patients still awaiting attention and one of these appeared to be keeping the others entertained by diagnosing his own complaint. Katy listened long enough to discover that he thought he had gangrene in his growth, wherever that might be, and long enough to hope that someone else would have the pleasure of dealing with him when his name was called.

She went to collect Mr Booker's card from the receptionist.

Mr Booker was lying down in a cubical, his face distorted with pain, clutching himself under the ribs. Katy was becoming suspicious of Mr Booker already. Mr Booker claimed to have been in great agony, under the ribs, for many hours, but he was showing few signs of exhaustion as a result of it. The young man who had just been sent up to Male Surgical with a perforated ulcer had waited in grey-faced anguish, reduced to total silence by his suffering, and total immobility. Mr Booker was writhing stylishly.

'Right,' said Katy, leaning over him and preparing to take notes. 'Can you tell me *exactly* what's happened?'

'Are you the Sister?' said Mr Booker.

The biggest nuisances always wanted the best attention.

'I'm afraid not,' said Katy. 'Doctor will be here to look at you in a minute, but he'd like to know what's happened before he starts.'

'It come on at work,' said Mr Booker.

'Where do you work?'

'Newbolt House; I'm on the door. It come on after lunch – just a sort of fluttering at first. And sore. A sort of soreness, all round the ribs, like they'd been skinned – inside.'

'And then?'

'Well, I sat down for a bit. And it went off. And then it came back strong; a tearing feeling, every time I breathe, like. Like all the ribs was broken off sharp and catching me lungs every time they went in and out.'

Katy pictured this unlikely situation.

'Anything like this happen before?'

'Never. Well, you know, the odd pain. They say a perfectly healthy person has at least one bad pain a day, don't they? But nothing like this. You know – I can feel the tearing, as though I was being scraped raw inside.'

'Have you been sick?'

'Ah.' He seemed to be weighing the pros and cons of having been sick. 'A bit, Nurse. Not much. But definitely sick.'

'When?'

'Today.'

'Before the pain started or after?'

'After – and before. A bit before and a bit after, actually.'

The doctor arrived, poked and questioned.

'Did that hurt?'

'Yes.'

'And this?'

'Yes.'

'Have you had any stomach trouble before?'

'Stomach?' said Mr Booker. 'I thought it was me breathing. I suppose I just feel it round there.'

'Any trouble?'

'Oh yes. Lots.'

Mr Booker was dispatched to the X-ray department.

'It won't be the year's most exciting photograph,' said the doctor, glumly, certain like Katy that Mr Booker, for some reason of his own, was passing the afternoon at their expense.

Katy went back to tidy the cubicle and was treated to a scrap of idle chat from two colleagues on the other site of the curtain, concerning Staff Nurse Gibbons from Maternity and Doctor Christodoulou, late owner of the Sprite. She listened avidly, dismayed to find that much as she hated to feel that she was the subject of gossip, she was as ready as anyone else to listen to gossip about other people. Her eavesdropping was rewarded by the mention of a third party.

'... and talking of naughty doctors, who do I see padding down the corridor like a tiger after his prey?'

'Evans, you mean? More like pussy after a sparrow.'

The voices drifted away. Katy looked out between the curtains and there *was* Hughie, hesitating on the other side.

'Excuse me,' said Katy, making as if to duck past him. Pussy after a sparrow, indeed. Only that was just what he looked like, and she was the sparrow.

'Just a minute,' said Hughie.

'What? I'm busy.' She noticed an unaccustomed wheedling tone in his voice that had never been there before.

'I know we agreed not to see each other for a bit —'

'Well?'

'That doesn't mean we have to avoid each other, does it?'

'That's about the only way of not seeing each other in this place.'

Hughie saw that wheedling was not going to work.

'Aren't you being rather foolish?' he said. 'We can't each go around pretending that the other doesn't exist.'

'You don't usually have any trouble doing that,' said Katy.

'I see,' said Hughie. 'You're the only one who's allowed to be hurt. It doesn't matter that *I'm* hurt too?'

'Are you?'

'I suppose it makes things easier for you if you pretend that I'm not.'

'Look,' said Katy, 'it would certainly make things easier for you if you stopped pretending that you were. I should go and have a look at Mr Booker, if I was you. He's just gone up to X-ray. He's a really good actor.'

'I see,' said Hughie.

'I don't think so,' said Katy. 'I don't think you do.'

7

Joanne put her head round the bedroom door.

'You're not staying in again, are you?'

Katy looked up from her notes.

'Why not? Mum's out, Kev's out, you're going out. It's the best night of the week to be in.'

'That's rich. I suppose we're not good enough for you, these days.'

'I didn't mean that, but it's quiet for once. I might get some work done.'

'I see you don't bring your Hughie here any more. Once was enough, eh?'

'I expect it was,' said Katy, sourly. Hughie's one visit to the flat had been enlivened by the presence of Bernard, Rachel, Jason and Mrs Lake. This crew, in addition to Granny having a turn in the living room while being introduced, had probably been enough to make him swear never to come near the place again.

Well, it was unlikely that he ever would come near the place again. Somehow the cooling-off period was turning colder and colder. She wanted to seek him out and tell him that it was time to think again, hoping that the coldness was all on her side, but she refused to go to him begging. He must be the beggar, and it seemed that he didn't know how to beg. If he didn't learn soon it would be too late.

'Have you seen Gran since you came in?' said Joanne.

'I looked in to say hullo, earlier, but she was watching *Blue Peter* so I crept out again. She never saw me. I didn't want to disturb her,' said Katy, innocently.

'She's had that pain again,' said Joanne. 'Mum said to tell you.'

'Look, I know she's old and her knees ache, and her back aches, and her hands shake,' said Katy, 'but I reckon that pain in her chest is one big con.'

'You mean she makes it up?'

'Oh no. *She* thinks she's got it, but have you noticed, it only comes on when we're all busy, or having dinner, or going out. Like, she never has it when you sit and watch telly with her, does she? We had a chap in Casualty a couple of days ago, with a pain in his chest. We all thought he was having us on but we had to make sure, didn't we? We couldn't just chuck him out, so he got examined, and X-rayed, and in the end he was admitted for observation. I asked how he was this morning and it turned out we were right. He *was* having us on. He just wanted to get away from his old lady for a few days. He'd told her a tale, see, and some friend had told her different, and he was afraid to go home. I mean, he must have been about fifty, and he was afraid to go home.'

'What's Gran supposed to be afraid of, then?' said Joanne, taking the point.

'Being on her own. Dying on her own, maybe,' said Katy. 'She's put a lot of work into getting a family together; now she wants some returns. She thinks we'll all stop worrying unless she gives us something to worry about.'

Joanne smiled. 'Poor old girl.'

'Yes, and never mind about poor old Katy,' Katy shouted, losing her temper. 'Why should I be the one who has to do all the worrying? No one else does a hand's turn while I'm here. There's nothing wrong with her. She just wants attention – I don't blame her – I'm not saying that – but any of you can make a fuss of her. It doesn't have to be me. She doesn't need a nurse, she needs company. If you weren't so idle you'd have seen that for yourself.'

Joanne went out, taking care not to slam the door. She had seen enough plays on television to know that icy calm was a more effective weapon than blind fury. Katy was past caring. She stuck cotton wool in her ears and opened her folder.

Casualty was over and done with for the time being. A fortnight on block and then she was stuck on Female Surgical for a couple of months. She hated working on a women's ward. Nothing but women for weeks and weeks and then exams at the end of it. And no Hughie.

Joanne slept on her back and snored, with the penetrating rasp of a powerful motorbike. Katy, sleeping badly, was roused in early morning darkness by Joanne revving up, and couldn't sleep again. She got out of bed and shook her sister who rolled over, mumbling into silence, but the damage was done. After trying to bore herself back to sleep by thinking about nothing, which was impossible these days, she put on her dressing gown and went into the kitchen hounded by thoughts of examinations, Hughie and the prospect of a long day's work after four hours' sleep.

She put the kettle on and after a few minutes Dad came up from the shop.

'You're about early,' he said, surprised to find her there.

'You can talk.' He had already been to market. 'I woke up ages ago – couldn't get back off again.'

'Did I make a row? Sorry, love,' he said, humbly. He was the quietest person in the flat and, it seemed to her, the only one with a conscience.

'It wasn't you, Dad. Jo blowing a gasket again. D'you want a cup?'

'I won't say no.'

'Here, we're out of tea bags. Does Mum know?'

'There's a quarter of the real stuff at the back of the cupboard, if you can remember how to use it.'

'Come off it, Dad.'

'Two spoonfuls and one for the pot. In the old days —'

'I know, you used to grow your own.'

They both laughed, but he peered at her, anxiously. 'You look tired. What time did you get to bed last night?'

'About ten – no – it must have been nearer eleven. But I was swotting for a couple of hours.'

'You work too hard.'

'You can talk,' she said, again. They settled on either side of the table with their cups of real tea.

'You don't get much social life, these days, do you?' he said. He looked into his tea cup while he waited for her answer. Katy wondered what he was expecting her to say.

'Not much. Still, it'll all be over in a few weeks. It'll be worth it then – that's what I tell myself, at any rate.'

'And what does your young man think about it?'

'Young man?' The phrase sounded so demure that for a moment she didn't know who he meant. 'Hughie?'

'That's it; Hughie. I couldn't think of his name for a minute.' He frowned into his tea. 'I must be getting old ... ought to be able to remember my own daughter's fiancé's name, oughtn't I? Perhaps if we saw more of him ...?' Katy knew he was seeking answers to questions that he hadn't the nerve to ask. 'You don't bring him here.'

'It's easier for me to go to his place, Dad.'

'So I've noticed.'

'Well, Dad, it's hard to – to entertain people here. With Gran and that.'

'If he comes to collect you or bring you home he never gets out of the car. That's not the only reason you go with him, is it?'

'What?'

'The car.'

'Of course not. Mind you, it's better than the back of a Honda —'

'Oh yes. Bobby Stokes. You were still at school. We soon had you off of that.'

'He's married with two kids now, Jo says. Anyway, I'm not "going with" Hughie. We're engaged.'

'Funny sort of engagement.' He ground his spoon into the sugar bowl. 'I was engaged to your mother for four years. All the time I was in the army – in Malaya – I hardly ever saw her, but we always wrote.'

'I don't have to write to Hughie. I see him all the time at work.'

'It might be better,' he said, 'if you didn't.' Katy wondered if he had guessed. 'It might help you make up your mind whether you really wanted him.' The spoon slipped and the sugar went flying in a gritty spray, all over the table.

'I have made up my mind, Dad.'

'Have you? You ought to talk to your Mum about this, not me. She could help you.'

'I don't need help.'

'I hope you're right,' he said, 'because you don't talk about him, do you? Seems to me you'd want to talk about him – you'd want *us* to talk about him, just to hear his name; but you don't. If we mention him you change the subject. I mean, you were always on about Bobby Stokes.'

'I was only a kid,' said Katy. 'It was just, well, just infatuation, like.'

'Well, I don't want you to be infatuated,' he said, gravely. 'But at least you were enjoying yourself, then. Strikes me you aren't very happy now.'

'No.'

'I don't want to interfere.'

'No, Dad. I never thought that.'

'That's all right then.' He dipped into his tea and brought out a short brown stalk. 'Here's a stranger. Haven't had a stranger in my tea for years.'

'You don't get strangers in tea bags.'

'You have him, love.' He passed her the stalk, very seriously. Katy put it on her thumb nail and flicked it away, as she had always done as a child. 'Now we just have to wait and see who turns up.'

'I got something for you,' said Elaine, and propped an envelope against the tomato ketchup bottle. 'Yuk; what have I stood it in? You'd think they'd wipe the tables occasionally, this place being so classy!' she said, raising her voice so that the manageress would hear. 'You got a tissue?'

Katy wiped the table and the envelope.

'Open it, then.'

The envelope contained a printed card with beribboned silver bells in one corner. Certain words stood out, written by hand: *Miss Kathleen Betts ... Dr Hugh Evans*: all very correct.

'It's an invite,' said Elaine. 'To my wedding. What's the matter? You wanted me to invite him, didn't you?'

'Yes. Thanks.' Katy went dredging for a smile. 'Thanks a lot, Elaine. I'll try and make it.'

'Try? What's all this? First you can't be a bridesmaid, now you can't come to the wedding.'

'I said I'd try —'

'You want to try a bit harder, mate.'

'Look, Elaine, I never promised. I said I'd try; I will try. It's just too far ahead to be certain.'

'That makes a change, at any rate,' said Elaine, bitterly.

'Oh yes? And what's that supposed to mean?'

'What do you think? I've heard of people living in the past – you live in the future. *One* day I'll be qualified. *One* day I'll apply for a job. *One* day I'll leave home. *One* day, ha, ha, I'll get married.'

'I expect I will,' said Katy, very coolly.

'*One* day. Well come to the wedding and make sure he comes too. It might make him buck his ideas up a bit. Anyway, I haven't met him yet.'

'Well, you aren't likely to, now.' Elaine's sulky face broke into a grin that was almost admiring.

'You've never given him the push?'

'I have, as a matter of fact,' said Katy. She had been dreading the moment when she confessed to Elaine that she no longer had a fiancé, knowing that Elaine already considered her deprived. But here was Elaine about to congratulate her, not even pretending to look sorry, which made a nice change from the gleeful sympathy dished out at St Angela's.

'I hope it was a good hard one,' said Elaine. 'Shut up.' She raised her hand. 'I know I never saw him. I didn't need to. He wasn't doing you any good, anyone could tell. You been looking like a wet weekend, lately.'

Katy actually found herself smiling. 'Oh no. Poor old Hughie. It's not all his fault.' How nice to be able to say poor old Hughie. How soothing. 'It's everything, really. The job, the money – well, no money, really – doing nights, trying to sleep at the flat. Trying to swot at the flat. It's quieter in Casualty on a Saturday night. I'm just all-over fed up.'

'You go on blaming Hughie,' said Elaine. 'It'll give you something to live for. I mean, you tell yourself *everything's* Hughie's fault and you'll stop noticing the rest. It won't matter. Go on; let him make himself useful for once.'

'Don't be rotten,' said Katy. 'I can't do that to him.'

'He won't know.'

'Look, I didn't get engaged just to pass the time; I thought I was going to get married. I loved him – still do, I suppose.' How strange *that* sounded. 'I wasn't just stringing him along.'

'Nah. He was just stringing you along. Better to worry about him than worry about your job. He'll take your mind off it. Anyway, I thought you said you were good at your work.'

'I am, but I still worry. I think you have to. You'd get too pleased with yourself otherwise. Then you start making mistakes.'

'I don't worry about my job.'

'Why should you?' said Katy. 'You can't kill anyone.'

'Can't I? Oops; sorry lady. Did I cut through your jugular by mistake? Never mind, with this style it won't show.'

'And I've got my assessment coming up.'

'Something you ate?'

'Don't be disgusting. No, assessment – like an exam. We have to do four, and this is the last.'

'Home and dry,' said Elaine.

'Not till I've done it. It's ward management, this time. You get left in charge, see, pretending like you're Sister, and the tutor goes round with you and you have to give her a report on every patient. And if there's a real emergency you still have to cope like you really were Sister. Still, there's one thing. They tell you right away whether you've passed or failed. You don't have to wait for weeks to find out.'

'How can you do that on Casualty?'

'I'm not on Casualty anymore,' said Katy. 'It'll be Female Surgical. I hate it. No one likes being on the women's wards.'

'I don't suppose the patients like it much, either,' said Elaine.

'One thing, though. I don't keep running into Hughie.'

'Start living for yourself, then,' Elaine advised. 'I don't like to see a girl crawling after a fella.'

'Better not look in the mirror, then,' said Katy.

8

'Mrs Ayers, you're crossing your ankles again,' said Katy, sternly.

Mrs Ayers looked up from her magazine with the same good-natured smile that she had been wearing since admission. She liked being in hospital and taking the weight off her feet. She had gone smiling to Theatre and Katy wouldn't mind betting that she had come round from the anaesthetic, still smiling.

'You told me to waggle my feet,' said Mrs Ayers, reasonably. She had not been waggling her feet.

'But not with your legs crossed.'

'It's easier.'

Katy went up to the head of the bed so as to have a better chance of competing with the magazine for Mrs Ayers's attention.

'You mustn't do it. If you were walking about you wouldn't need to be waggling your feet, would you? You'd be getting all the exercise you need.'

'Yes, dear.'

'But you need to do the exercises because you *aren't* walking about. And if you lie still with your legs crossed, it undoes all the good work.'

Mrs Ayers nodded and looked down at her magazine again.

'Mrs Ayers; the physiotherapist told you, didn't she? She explained.'

'Yes, dear.'

'Didn't you understand?'

'She's so busy. I didn't like to ask her to go ali through it again.'

'You should have asked us if there was anything you wanted to know. We're here to help you get better.'

'Yes, well, you're all so busy too.'

Katy closed in. 'Look, love, it's no use us being busy if you don't get better, is it? We're busy making you better, aren't we? Or trying to.' She thought, I sound like something out of *Doctor Ballantyne's Secret.* I'd really like to kick the silly old bat.

'Yes, dear.'

'If you just lie there without moving you could develop a blood clot.'

'Thrombosis, Sister said,' remarked Mrs Ayers, with maddening complacency.

'Well, a thrombosis isn't something you want,' said Katy, trying hard not to snarl. 'It would be worse than varicose veins.'

'I haven't got varicose veins,' said Mrs Ayers. 'I had them stripped. I was on this same ward, too, but it was a couple of years ago. You weren't here then.'

'I said it would be worse than varicose veins,' said Katy swiftly. 'And if you've had surgery before you should know why you have to do the exercises. Your leg could swell right up – even a light touch would hurt terribly.' It was like threatening a disobedient child who wouldn't listen. 'And that could lead to complications.'

'Dying, you mean?'

'Possibly. A pulmonary embolism.' Since you prefer long words, thought Katy.

'Doctor said I could go home on Friday.'

'You won't be able to go home with a pulmonary embolism, will you?'

Mrs Ayers's eyes were sliding down towards the magazine again. She was looking at a page of advertisements for the kind of shoes she hadn't been able to wear for years.

'Have you been doing your breathing exercises?'

'Oh yes.' The smile flashed brighter than ever.

Katy sighed pointedly, with no result.

'I think I'd better get Sister to have a word with you.'

'That's right, dear.'

Katy moved away. Mrs Ayers leaned over to her neighbour and remarked, 'She's young enough to be my daughter. She sounds like my mother, the way she goes on.'

Katy kept moving.

'They treat you like idiots,' said the neighbour. Mrs Ayers went back to her magazine, ankles crossed.

'Look, Gran, just because you've got pins and needles, it doesn't mean you've got air in your veins,' said Katy.

'I keep going numb underneath,' said Gran.

'You should try to move about more. I showed you how to do the exercises,' said Katy, with a deadly feeling of having been through all this before.

'Wait till you get to my age and see how much you feel like doing exercises,' said Gran. 'You'll have me up on the asymmetric bars next.' She had been watching a gymnastic display. Now that was over she was rousing herself with a few wrestling bouts before tea. Frightful grunts and snorts came from the television set. 'Now where are you going?'

'Back to bed,' said Katy.

'But it's only four o'clock.'

'It's the middle of the night, for me,' said Katy. 'I've got to go to work at half past nine.'

'Well who's going to sit with me? I've been on me own all afternoon.'

'I'll see if Kevin's home.'

'He's no good. He keeps going away. You don't want me

to get depressed, do you?' said Gran, ominously.

'Who says you'll get depressed?'

Joanne looked in at the door, saw that Katy was there and started to sneak out again.

'No need to go,' said Katy.

'Mum said to see how Gran was. No need to stay if you're here.'

'I'm just going back to bed. Hey —' Katy noticed the corner of a familiar magazine sticking out from under the bed. 'That's my *Nursing Mirror*. What's it doing in here?'

'I thought Gran might like to look at it,' said Joanne.

Katy scooped up the magazine and pursued Joanne into the kitchen.

'What you want to go and give her this for?'

'I thought it might cheer her up.'

'Cheer her up? *This?*'

'She enjoys them horrible pictures, doesn't she?'

'That's where she's getting all her ideas from, you stupid cow,' said Katy. 'She's been reading up the symptoms. What's this care study? Endogenous depression? She thinks she's got that now. I thought you'd have more sense, Jo.'

'How was I to know?' said Joanne, aggrieved. 'I didn't think she read it. I told you, she just likes looking at the pictures, horrible things.'

'She's not an idiot,' said Katy. 'Just because she's old doesn't mean there's anything wrong with her brain.'

Joanne back-pedalled, rapidly. 'I mean, I didn't think she'd understand it – with all those long medical words.'

'You didn't think at all, if you ask me,' said Katy. 'D'you want to frighten her to death, because you're going the right way about it. Go and do something useful for once. Make her a cup of tea and go and sit with her.'

'She doesn't want me. She's glued to that telly all day long. She don't talk or anything.'

'That's got nothing to do with it,' said Katy. 'She wants someone with her.'

'You sit with her then.'

'I'm going back to bed. I've had one hour's sleep and I'm on again tonight.' Katy felt herself beginning to cry through sheer anger. Joanne stared.

'All right. I'll make her some tea. I'll bring you a cup and all, shall I?' It was a rare peace offering, but Katy shook her head.

'No. Thanks. Just let me go to bed and let me stay there. That's the nicest thing you can do for me. And give Kev a clip round the ear if he turns on his hi-fi, because if I get to him first ...'

'You'll be doing us all a favour,' said Joanne.

Katy's ward management assessment proceeded without incident. Only three patients remained to be reported upon; Mrs Lucas, Mrs Ayers and Miss Thackeray. Barbara Marshall, the second-year student, who was currently arguing with Miss Thackeray, called them the Three Billy Goats Gruff, the Three Weird Sisters or, in less charitable moments, the Unholy Trinity. Katy had to approach them with less literary ammunition. She loathed them impartially and therefore had to save her sweetest smiles for that end of the ward. She wouldn't put it past Mrs Ayers to have her pulmonary embolism right now, in the middle of the assessment, just as Katy was telling the tutor how well Mrs Ayers was progressing.

Miss Thackeray consulted a nursing manual at intervals and told anyone who would listen that she was receiving the wrong treatment. Mrs Ayers declined to walk anywhere, except to the lavatory, and continued to sneak back to bed when she could, still with her ankles crossed. Mrs Lucas was a model patient, as regards her own operation, but the other two called her in as a kind of expert witness when they wanted their opinions reinforced. Mrs Lucas's command of English was small. When appealed to she smiled and said, 'Yaas, thaas right,' regardless of the original remark. Ayers and Thackeray knew when they were on to a good thing.

'And this patient?' said the tutor, halting at the foot of Mrs Ayers's bed.

'Ankles, Mrs Ayers,' said Katy, with a brilliant smile. 'This is Mrs Ayers, who was operated on for a peptic ulcer last Monday. She is due to be discharged on Friday. She was found to be slightly anaemic on admission and was given a blood transfusion. The sutures were removed from the wound yesterday and the patient is very cheerful and making excellent progress except —' Katy fixed Mrs Ayers with a beady eye '— she is very reluctant to take any exercise. She was visited by the physiotherapist after she recovered consciousness and it was explained to her that breathing and leg exercises were essential to reduce the risk of deep venous thrombosis. We also tried to explain what would happen if she *did* develop a thrombosis, but Mrs Ayers,' said Katy, forgetting the formalities, 'reckons that being in hospital is a good chance to put her feet up for a bit, and she may not get another so she's making the best of it.'

'Yaas, thaas right,' said Mrs Lucas, under the impression that she had been consulted.

'Also,' said Katy, lowering her voice, 'the patient in the last bed, Miss Thackeray, who has undergone an exploration of the common bile duct, has got a very old book about nursing which she keeps under the pillow. She told Mrs Ayers that she ought to be on complete bed rest.'

'I see. And how is Miss Thackeray treating herself?'

'Miss Thackeray talks of discharging herself.'

'I see. And what advice have you to offer Miss Thackeray?'

'We've tried to reassure Miss Thackeray that she is receiving the proper treatment, but she is unwilling to believe any of the nursing staff, or the doctor. She says she only came in here because her brother talked her into it. She lives alone and if she does discharge herself there will be no one at home to look after her. We have asked the medical social worker to look into the situation, but Miss Thackeray says that we are going to get a mental health order and have her put away.'

'Is the patient confused?'

'I don't think so,' said Katy. 'Just used to getting her own way. She likes arguing. I mean, she'll be discharged in a couple of days, anyway. If she's going to discharge herself she'd better get a move on.'

'Thaas right,' said Mrs Lucas.

'I passed it!' said Katy. 'I passed, I passed, and old mother Ayers didn't die on me. And Thackeray didn't get up and walk out. That's it. I've finished. No more assessments.'

'You qualified now?' said Elaine. 'What do they give you, a gold bedpan?'

'No, I'm not qualified,' said Katy. 'I've got the written exams now. Hospital finals, and then State finals, and I've got to find a job ...'

'You enjoy looking on the black side, don't you?' said Elaine. 'One thing at a time, I say. And first things first. Thirst things first – Chris told me that. What are you having?'

Katy looked across the bar. The rear wall was covered by a mirror and the bottles and glasses were arranged on mirror tiles in front of it. Very nice if you're seeing double already, thought Katy. 'I'll have a snowball,' she said.

'No you won't. That's for Christmas and ladies-only coach parties,' said Elaine. 'This is a celebration. Have a short.'

'I'd rather not. They're not what I call a drink. They go down too fast and if you drink them slowly they taste horrible. Do you think they do port and lemon?'

'And that's for funerals,' said Elaine. 'Have a rum and blackcurrant.'

'It looks like meths,' said Katy, when Elaine came back with the drink.

'I don't know why you don't hang yourself and have done with it,' said Elaine. 'Cheers. Likewise, Skal, Prosit and L'chayim,' she said, reading it off the beer mat. 'What's all this about a job?'

'Look, I got to get out of that flat,' said Katy. 'I mean, I got a smashing family, I know that. I'll do anybody that says different, but they're – so – bleeding – noisy. Mum thinks I'll go on living there till I get married. Well, that was all right, only I'm not getting married now. I can't get any work done. I can't sleep. I've got to get out.'

'Can't you live in the nurses' home?'

'Not with my family just round the corner. They're already short of space as it is. Anyway, if I leave home it'll be so I can do *what* I like *when* I like, without half the hospital knowing about it. I had thought of trying for Wandsworth, but I don't know. It's so close. I might go over the river.'

'Gor, that's daring,' said Elaine. 'It's all of three hundred yards. Why don't you get right out of London?'

'I couldn't live in the country,' said Katy. 'You know, this *tastes* like meths, too. It'd be all tetanus and fingers lopped off in the combine harvester, or whatever they pick spuds with.'

'It's not all country out there, you know,' said Elaine. 'It's not green fields all the way to the edge. Most of it looks like Battersea, from what I've seen. There's other towns besides London.'

'Gravesend?'

'No, seriously. What about, well . . .' Her geography failed her. 'Leeds? Or Manchester or Birmingham?'

'Manchester?' said Katy. '*Leeds?* I know someone from Leeds. It's a foreign country, mate. They don't even talk English.'

9

'Listen,' said Katy. 'Listen. *Please.* Everyone listen.'

For once everybody, except the canary and the gerbils, did listen. They looked up from the table, open mouthed, and Katy was so surprised that she forgot what she was going to say.

'Well, get on with it then,' said Mrs Betts. 'It was you we were supposed to listen to, wasn't it?'

'I've got my exams tomorrow,' said Katy. 'My hospital finals.'

'Big deal,' said Kevin.

'About time,' said Joanne. 'We've heard enough about your exams —'

'Just listen,' said Katy. 'I want to work tonight. Revision. And I don't want to listen to the telly, or the hi-fi, or the radio. And I don't want to have to go in to Gran half a dozen times. And when I've finished revising I want to go to bed early, and sleep all night, and get up in the morning feeling half-way human instead of like something that's been brought in for a wash-out. OK?'

'Anything else, madam?' said Mum.

'I didn't mean to yell,' said Katy, although in this household that was one thing you need never apologize for. 'But I mean it. You don't want me to fail?'

'I get it. If you fail it'll be our fault.'

'Well, no one's been exactly helpful, have they?' said Katy. She closed the door on them and went back to the bedroom.

The family began to cooperate with the best intentions.

For a while Katy could hear nothing but the sound of washing up as the crockery left over from mid-day was removed from the sink to make room for the supper things. Joanne came in to fetch her coat and while the door was open Katy heard a little discreet music from the radio in the kitchen, and an occasional subdued quack from Gran's television, but nothing more.

'Where's Kev?' she asked, suspiciously.

'Cleaning out the gerbils,' said Joanne. 'You put the fear of God into him just now.'

'Just as well, they were beginning to smell,' said Katy. 'Going anywhere nice, are you?'

'Disco. Why don't you come? It'll take your mind off of things. You ought to relax before an exam. I always did.'

'Yes, and look where it got you. Grade Three Needlework,' said Katy.

Joanne flounced out, giving the door a tremendous slam so that it opened again and hit the dressing table. Katy got up and closed it, but the crash seemed to have given people ideas. Imperceptibly, the radio in the kitchen became louder, and Gran turned up the television so as to be able to hear it above the radio. Then Mum turned up the radio so as to be able to hear it above the television and Kevin began to shout in order to be heard at all. The front door banged as Joanne went out. Kevin finished with the gerbils and went upstairs.

Katy listened to him go up. 'If you touch that hi-fi,' she muttered. 'If you just touch it ... so much as lay a finger on it ...'

Suddenly it was impossible to concentrate. Kevin did not switch on the hi-fi, but at any moment he *might*. Katy found that she had stopped reading and was lying on the bed, rigid with expectation, and ready to go charging upstairs at the very first thud.

What on earth was he doing?

The tension became unbearable. Katy put down her notes and went upstairs, ever so quietly. Half way up she became aware of an eerie moan that eddied round the stair well like wind among haunted ruins. Kevin was sitting on the floor, surrounded by the guts of his hi-fi system which now occupied every spare surface. Red robot eyes glowed in the darkness. Needles flickered across dials. The amplifier groaned to itself as though in unbearable pain.

'How can you afford all that stuff?' Katy asked enviously, ducking under a taut wire that traversed the room at exactly the right height to slice off an unwary head. 'It's not hot is it?'

'No it isn't,' said Kevin, righteously offended. 'It's bits of old ones, mostly. I put it together myself – me and Mick Hoskins.'

'I don't know him. Who is he, a fence?'

'His brother,' said Kevin impressively, 'works for South Bank Sounds, in the precinct. He helps us.' He held up a disc to the light and tut-tutted old-womanishly over greasy finger prints. 'Eeeeech, look at this.' He fetched a velvet preener from the drawer and lovingly anointed the grooves. Katy recognized the record as one of her own, that Hughie had returned. That was Hughie's own greasy finger print that Kevin was wiping away. There was something very terminal about that.

'Your records get intensive care, I see,' said Katy.

'People who can't look after them shouldn't have them,' said Kevin. He lowered the record on to the turntable, but as he touched his fingers to the arm the moan of the amplifier was cut short in an outraged belch. He switched off hurriedly and turned to consult his Bible, the heap of pamphlets and pages torn from technical manuals that littered the bed.

'You got trouble?' said Katy.

'Yeah.'

'Right, well, so've I.'

'You said, already.'

'I'm just reminding you,' said Katy. 'You've got a short memory. I mean, my room's right underneath. I don't just hear your music, I *feel* it. Can't you wear your earphones?'

'Headphones,' said Kevin, absentmindedly. He had found the data he was seeking and was all set to rip the back off the amplifier.

Katy edged out, watching for live wires, and closed the door. Up the stairs rolled the sound of the radio from the kitchen, back at its normal volume, and the sound of Gran's television, louder than ever. Gran's programme had a cackling canned audience. The canary had hysterics.

Katy went down, closed all the doors that could be closed, and retired to the back bedroom, where she found Joanne crouched over the dressing table.

'I thought you went out.'

'Well, I came back, didn't I?'

'What happened to the disco?'

'Had a row with Dave, didn't I?' said Joanne, in a foul temper. Since the errant Dave was out of reach she wreaked her vengeance on the dressing table, opening drawers and slamming them shut.

'Are you going to do that all evening?'

'What if I do?'

'There's plenty of drawers in the kitchen. Try the one with the knives and forks in, it makes more row.'

Joanne took the hint and settled down to tweezer out the last rogue hairs from her eyebrows.

'Here, Katy, is this a blackhead?'

'If it is, I don't want to see it,' said Katy. She sat down on the bed, reopened her folder and simultaneously the sound of synthesizers oozed through the ceiling, accompanied by the thud of boots stamping out an enthusiastic percussion.

Katy fled up the stairs again and burst into Kevin's room, heedless of danger. Kevin was gyrating, waving a screwdriver; technician and rhythm section in one person.

'Can't you just shut it for five minutes?' Katy yelled, above the synthesizer.

'Eh?'

She stabbed a finger towards the pamphlets.

'Haven't you got one that tells you how to turn the sound down?'

'Eh?'

'Can you hear me?'

'What?'

Katy advanced on the amplifier, seized the nearest festoon of flex and tugged.

There was the most beautiful silence.

Katy bent low over the table, as if on starting blocks, gripped her pen in a sweaty hand and waited for the word to begin. It was like GCE all over again, and she had sworn then that she would never take another exam, ever. It was the smell that did it; not a hospital smell but the pervasive odour of Gestetner ink. It had been with her all morning while she tried to place it, aware of it even while she worked her way through the three-hour exam paper.

Strange how three hours disappeared when you were working against the clock. Strange how they dragged when you wanted them gone, like on night duty, or, more relevantly, like the GCE History exam, which she had failed. That hadn't been anything like three hours, but it had felt like ten and she remembered with shame the miserable little answers she had fudged up in reply to the cruel questions. She had sat for half an hour doing nothing at all, and then wrote three lines for the last answer, so that it would look as though she had been so pressed for time that she had been unable to finish, instead of being very nearly unable to start. It had fooled no one.

Well, that was a long time ago, and this was very different. She had enjoyed herself this morning. The panic had subsided as soon as she turned over the paper. There were five questions to be answered out of eight and she could have chosen any of them. She had, however, left out the one about amputation.

A middle-aged housewife is admitted to your ward for an above-knee amputation of the leg, as a result of a road accident. Describe in detail the pre-operative care up to the time you hand over the patient to the theatre staff . . .

My patient wasn't admitted to the ward. She was lying in the ruins of a restaurant with a beam across her legs. We were choking with dust. The ceiling was about to collapse on us. I was as frightened as she was. Pre-operative care? I talked to her. I cried.

There were no theatre staff. There was no theatre. I couldn't set her mind at rest. She was screaming when they gave her the anaesthetic.

Post-operative care. I sat beside my patient and held her hand. She said she was glad I stayed with her.

Supposing I had written about that; would I have got any marks?

Please, no questions about amputation in the multi-choice . . .

A voice at the front of the room said, 'Turn over your papers and begin.'

'Finished then, have you?' said Mum, looking up from her pools coupon. 'We can all relax now.'

'I didn't notice anyone *not* relaxing,' said Katy.

'How'd you get on?' said Dad.

'Well, I suppose it's unlucky to say I did all right, but I don't think I did so badly. But you can't tell, really. There was this question about potassium salts in an intravenous infusion —'

'It's no good telling me,' said Mrs Betts. 'You know that. I don't know what you're on about. There, that's it. Will you post this when you go out?'

'Where are you going?' said Joanne.

'Round Elaine's. We're going for a drink, to celebrate.'

'I should save your celebrating till you've passed,' said Joanne. 'I don't know why you hang around with that Elaine. She never comes here if she can help it.'

'It's nice to see someone who's not at the hospital,' said Katy. 'Anyway, it won't all be celebrating. I've got to tell her I can't make it to the wedding. She's going to be narked about that.'

'I thought that was all fixed up,' said Mrs Betts.

'It was, but they postponed it for a fortnight, and I can't get that Saturday off. It's not my fault but she won't like it. Still, I've got the whole week off before, so I can help her with her shopping.'

'That's not my idea of a holiday,' said Joanne. 'You can go shopping any old time. Why don't you go away somewhere?'

'Nowhere to go and no one to go with.'

'If I was you I'd find someone to go with, now you've got that Hughie out of your hair. He gave me the creeps that time he was round here,' said Joanne, who hadn't dared say what she thought of Hughie while Katy was still engaged, and was now making up for lost time. 'He kept looking at us like he wished he'd brought his rubber gloves along.'

'There's no need to make remarks about him,' said Katy. 'We just weren't suited, that's all.'

'You can call it that if you like,' said Joanne, darkly.

'In any case,' said Katy, changing the subject in a hurry, 'I can't afford to go anywhere.'

'Your cousin Pat'd be glad to have you for a week,' said Dad.

'I bet she would,' said Katy. 'So I can look after her screaming kids. No thanks. Tell you what, though, I was thinking of looking round for a job.'

'Instead of nursing?' said Joanne. 'You left it a bit late, didn't you?'

'No, something part-time, in the evenings, or something.'

'I thought you weren't supposed to do that,' said her mother.

'We aren't, but everybody does. Moonlighting. A lot of the girls go as Agency nurses when they're off-duty, but I can't do that till I'm Registered. Barbara – on my ward – she's been working as a barmaid.'

'No reason why you shouldn't then,' said Mrs Betts. 'Unless that's not good enough for you, these days. Ian and Dora are looking for someone to help out at The Feathers, three nights a week. Whyn't you go and see them?'

'I might.' Katy hadn't expected to have the matter of choice taken out of her hands so suddenly. She had only lately been considering the idea of moonlighting in any case, but why not? And why not The Feathers? She had known Ian and Dora for years. Dora was her godmother and the pub was popular locally. It might be a way of getting in touch with the old crowd again, and even if it wasn't, it meant money. Hard cash. Filthy lucre. Call it what you like, she needed it.

'I can't see you as a barmaid,' said Elaine. 'Barmaids are supposed to be fat and happy.'

'I'll be happy all right, if I'm earning some money,' said

Katy. 'Soon as I get this settled I going to apply for a post. If I can get a bit of money behind me I might be able to afford a flat – if I can find someone to share with.'

'You still on about that?' said Elaine.

'I mean it. I didn't tell you about that row I had with Kev last night, over his hi-fi. He wouldn't turn it down, so I pulled all the wires out the back. I didn't mean to, I just couldn't stick the racket any longer. I got my ears blasted for that, and then Gran wanted her back rubbed. I hardly got any revising done in the end. I can't go on like that. Tell you what, though, I did all right today, even without the revision.'

'Counting chickens ...' Elaine warned.

'I mean, I wouldn't have done any better if I'd sat up revising all night. Some of those multi-choice questions were tricky, though.'

'I don't want to hear nothing nasty,' said Elaine, 'so save your breath.'

'Well, work this one out. A patient collapses and dies in the bath. What would you do first? Tell the Doctor, tell the Sister, pull out the plug, start mouth to mouth resuscitation or get him out of the bath?'

'Call the undertakers,' said Elaine.

'No, be serious. After the heart stops you've got four minutes before brain damage occurs. You can't just leave him.'

'I could,' said Elaine. 'And thinking about it don't improve the flavour of the beer. Forget your exams for a bit and enjoy yourself.'

'All right.' Katy finished her drink. 'Get that down you and we'll go along to The Feathers.'

'Some celebration,' said Elaine. 'Don't you think about anything but work?'

10

The Feathers was conveniently close to home; down the road and round the corner, near the railway arches. Its real name was The Prince of Wales, but no one knew which Prince it referred to, so the sign outside just showed The Prince of Wales's feathers, and that was what everyone called it. Strangers asking for The Prince of Wales got a blank look from the locals.

Dora exactly fitted Elaine's description of a barmaid; fat and happy. Ian, the Guv'nor, was happy and so were the customers, but it took Katy a little while to discover if she were happy too. In the end she decided that she was, in spite of her earlier misgivings, the result of having worked as a waitress for a month when she left school. It had been enough to put her off the catering trade for life.

'Two coffees, Miss.'

'Four coffees, Miss.'

'Egg and chips twice, Miss.'

'We've been here half an hour already, *Miss.*'

But in The Feathers it was Darling.

'Two pints, Darling.'

'A Guinness and a rum and coke, Darling.'

And often, 'What'll you have, Darling?'

Katy stuck to halves of lager and lime and preferred the public bar to the saloon, where the customers, on the rarer occasions that they offered, seemed to think that she would want what they wanted, which nearly always had gin in it.

One evening she was drying glasses with her back turned to the bar when a voice behind her said, 'Two pints of bitter, Nurse.' She looked up quickly, all guilty conscience, and in the mirror behind the optics saw Hughie leering through the blue fume that hung like a curtain between the ceiling and the bar.

She had seen very little of Hughie since the day she gave him back his ring, and when she did see him he gave her nothing more than a distant smile as though she were a barely remembered patient. She knew now that she had hurt him. At the time it had seemed impossible that she should be able to, and she had never intended it, but looking back she saw that it was inevitable that he should be hurt. His pride was wounded if not his feelings. She had wondered sometimes, in the early days of their engagement, that he should think her good enough for him. By giving him the boot she had publicly declared that in her opinion he wasn't good enough for her. As she looked at his face in the mirror she saw that he hadn't forgiven her, and also that he was drunk, or very nearly. Surely he hadn't come on purpose to plague her?

'Hullo, Hughie. I haven't seen you in here before.'

'I haven't been in here before,' said Hughie, 'but word was going around that there was a fanciable filly in The Feathers, worth giving the once-over, so I came along. You know my nose for talent. I didn't know it would be you.'

'Pull the other one,' said Katy.

'See what a welcome I get,' said Hughie, over his shoulder and Katy observed that he had company; a wiry young man, nearer her age than his, with a drooping moustache that made him look like an urban guerrilla. 'We'd like two pints of whatever passes for best bitter in this neck of the woods.'

'Introssuce uss,' said the moustache, swimming towards the bar.

'This is Katy Betts,' said Hughie. 'My ex-fiancée. A

small thing and not even mine own. Katy, this is Cedric. He's into teeth.'

'What?'

'Denssissry,' said Cedric, having trouble with his own teeth. He found the bar and leaned on it gratefully. 'Guys.'

'Come along Nurse; chop-chop,' said Hughie.

'Don't call me that here.'

'Oh, you're in good company. Cedric moonlights too. Tell her what you do, Cedric.'

Katy took another look at Cedric and guessed that it might be body-snatching. Hughie, seeing that Cedric could have difficulty locating his hip pocket, delved in and brought out a business card, mangled and badly sat on.

NIGHT MANOEUVRES: REMOVALS CO-OP:
FRIENDLY DRIVERS

'He's a friendly driver?'

'He's extremely friendly, aren't you, Cedric?' said Hughie. 'Dentists make great removal men – it comes from pulling teeth all day. Heave-ho and up she rises. They have very strong right arms.'

''cept the left-handed ones,' said Cedric, cleverly.

'I shouldn't like to be one of his patients tomorrow,' said Katy. 'I hope he's not driving, tonight,' she added, severely.

'Is that why you won't serve us?'

'And I hope you're not driving tonight.'

'We have a sober friend down the road,' said Hughie. 'Now are we going to get our drinkies or do I have to tell Sister?'

'Oh, give it a rest.' Katy brought out two glasses from under the bar. 'Which do you want; fined bitter or Honest John?'

'Since they are sure to be equally nasty I'll let you choose,' said Hughie.

'Then you'll get the dear one and like it,' said Katy.

Cedric took his pint, slopped the head over his hand and the next couple of inches over the bar top, and began to subside on to a stool where he folded up until his chin was resting on a beer mat that floated by.

'What's he going to do – syphon it up his nose?' said Dora, in passing. 'Are they giving you any trouble, dear?'

'Not at the moment,' said Katy, looking hard at Hughie and seeing what Dora saw; not Hughie, not Doctor Evans, not even her ex-fiancé, but just one more tiresome customer with a legless friend; and she wished he would go away.

'You're not revising again, are you?' said Joanne, entering the bedroom warily.

'Looking for a job.'

'I thought you'd gone after one already.'

'Yes, well, if I don't get it, and I probably shan't, I shall have to apply for another. So I might as well do it now. I can't just sit around and wait till I get my results. Anyway, I'm not sure that I want that job at Wandsworth. It's too close to home,' said Katy, incautiously.

'Fed up with us, are you?'

'I wouldn't mind a change. Anyway, Jo, don't pretend you'd mind seeing me move out. You can't enjoy sharing a room any more than I do.'

'It's a bind when you're on nights,' Joanne admitted.

'That doesn't stop you coming in.'

'But we have to keep remembering to be quiet.'

'I can't say I've noticed. Wouldn't *you* like a place of your own?'

'I dunno. You'd have to share, even so, wouldn't you? You never know what might turn up.'

'There's a girl at the hospital,' said Katy, 'she lives quite close as a matter of fact, she advertised for someone to share her flat and look after her kid. It didn't work out, but she was desperate. She had to take the first person she could get. I wouldn't be that badly off for a start.'

She turned over the situations vacant pages at the back of the *Nursing Times*. *'Happy nursing in Ramsgate'*; *'Expanding Northampton, room to develop your talents'*; *'Tayside, area of opportunity.'*

'Jo, where's Tayside?'

'I dunno. Beside the Tay, I expect.'

'Thanks for nothing.' Katy went into the kitchen and borrowed Kevin's atlas that he had brought from school in order to do his homework. He was watching television and made no protest when she took it away.

'Tayside's in Scotland. Look up Northampton, will you?'

'I thought you did Geography for O-Level,' said Joanne.

'Geography's not much help when you want to know where places are. *"Are you bored with general ward work? Do you want variety and a chance to —"* No, that's no good. They want an SEN; anyway, I'm not bored with general ward work.'

'How's this sound?' Joanne couldn't resist a magazine, no matter what it was about, and she began to forage on her own account. '*"Active sports and social club. Single accommodation."* That's what you want, isn't it?'

'Yes, but what's the job?'

'*"Night Sister/Charge Nurse. Minimum qualifications:* SRN *with experience as Staff Nurse."* That's not you, is it?'

'Not quite. Keep looking for Staff vacancies.'

'What's a Charge Nurse?'

'That's not me, either. It's a Sister, only it's a man.'

Joanne, for some reason, thought this was funny. 'You couldn't call a man Sister, could you? Why not Brother? Why are Sisters called Sister, anyway?'

'I suppose it's left over from the time when they were all nuns. I don't know. St Angela was a nun.'

'You're a bit of a nun yourself these days, if you ask me,' said Joanne.

'I didn't ask you,' said Katy. 'Look up Stockport while you're at it.'

'You haven't had a fella since you ditched Horrible Hughie. It's in Cheshire. You'll do yourself an injury.'

'Just because I don't tell you every time I go out with a bloke . . .'

'I don't mean going out,' said Joanne. 'You know what I mean.'

'I've got enough to think of without getting tied down again,' said Katy. 'All I'm bothered about at the moment is getting my finals and getting a job. Anything else I do is just to pass the time. Get it?'

'Got it. What about this one? *"There is a vacancy in our A & E department for an* SRN *who seeks experience as a Staff Nurse. Single accommodation."* It's in Berkshire.'

'Right out in the sticks.'

'What, all of it?'

'As far as I'm concerned, everything's sticks that isn't London – or Brum, maybe. I don't mind having a go at Birmingham. See what they've got.'

Joanne droned on: 'Harrow, Hants, Middlesex – that's London, almost – Sidcup, Solihull. This one tells you the money. £2646–£3255.'

'Which one?'

'Solihull.'

'No thanks.'

Katy applied for the Wandsworth post and wrote away for ten other application forms.

'You're not going after them all, are you?' said Joanne, watching Katy stick on stamps.

'I'm hedging my bets,' said Katy. 'No pun intended, so don't bother to say anything. When you ask for an application form they send you a job description as well. You can't really tell what it'll be like till you've seen that.'

'That's nearly a quid gone, just on stamps,' said Joanne, awed by such all-out determination. 'You're really getting business-like, aren't you?'

'Elaine said I was getting efficient.'

'Well, it's not an insult,' said Joanne, which was as near as she had ever come to paying a compliment. 'Can you believe those job descriptions though? I mean, they're not going to tell you if you'll be working in a pre-fab between the brewery and the gas-works, are they? No one would apply.'

'They want nurses, not beauty councillors,' said Katy. 'They don't tell you the hours are short and the money's good, either, do they? You *know* that the hours are long and the money's bad and the food's lousy. You *know* you're going to be worn out and your feet ache. I mean, you *know*. It doesn't matter where you go, it'll always be the same.'

'I should go full-time at The Feathers,' Joanne advised. 'You'll still get lousy money and aching feet. I suppose that's what they call job satisfaction.'

'You're getting to sound like Elaine,' said Katy. 'I'll post these on the way to work. D'you want anything sent off?'

'You're not on nights again?' said Joanne. 'I lose count.'

'No, lates. Male Medical,' said Katy.

'I thought you were doing the old ladies now.'

'I was, more's the pity. I like Geriatric,' said Katy, conscious that nursing old ladies in the geriatric ward was far more rewarding than nursing Granny. She hoped that this wasn't because she got paid for nursing the old ladies in the geriatric ward. 'But they're short staffed on Male Medical, so I got moved. I'm barrier nursing at the moment.'

'What's barrier nursing? Standing outside and handing things in through the window?'

'You're asking a lot of questions lately,' said Katy. 'You never used to be interested. Not so long ago you said it made you sick. You're not changing your mind, are you?'

'What's barrier nursing?'

'You're never thinking of nursing, yourself, are you? After seeing me at it? You'd have to cut out the long green nails for a start. Anyway, you argue too much. You'd always think that things were being done the wrong way.'

'Supposing they were? You wouldn't just keep your mouth shut, would you?'

'You'd have to be pretty sure before you said anything. Sister wouldn't thank you for telling her she didn't know her job,' said Katy. 'Still, it's a bit different with barrier nursing —'

'What *is* barrier nursing?'

'Well, my patient's got meningitis,' said Katy. 'It's very infectious so he has to be isolated; very quiet, darkened room. He's on his own, in a side ward; he needs a lot of attention – I have to do everything for him. I know more about him than anyone. If anything was being done wrong then I'd know, because I'd be the one doing it. I have to do four-hour observations, wash him, turn him, feed him and watch him, all the time.'

'Is he paralysed?'

'Oh no,' said Katy, 'but he's not properly conscious yet.'

'What's he like?'

'Hard to tell. About my age.'

'Oh, young.' Joanne looked sentimental. 'Is he nice?'

'He's very ill,' said Katy. 'That's all I've noticed. That's all that matters. Are you interested, Jo? Really? I could tell you more.'

'It's all right. That's enough to be going on with.'

'Were you really thinking about training?' Katy grew enthusiastic, in spite of herself. 'I know you haven't got O-Levels but you could go for an SEN. Shall I —'

'Don't worry,' said Joanne. 'It's not for me. It's my friend Jackie. She's hooked on the idea.'

'You want to help her?'

'No fear. I'm trying to talk her out of it.'

The meningitis case, who had collapsed in the street carrying no means of identification, turned out to be a student called Richard Knowles. Katy was glad to know his name at last, although he never answered to it. He lay quite flat in his darkened room and followed her movements through half-closed eyelids.

She knew that it was the matter-of-fact necessities – her gown and mask, the silence, the darkness, all the things that she took for granted – that frightened him most, although his first miserable panic had subsided to a quiet and chronic distress.

She could only guess at the dismay caused by the indistinct sight of a faceless figure that appeared and disappeared in the half light; probing, handling, turning him, so she talked while she was with him, in a voice that her family would never have recognized, as much to herself as to him.

'You want the curtains open? I don't think you do, really. It's very bright outside – it would hurt your eyes. A headache's the last thing . . . I'm going to take your temperature now, and your pulse. Yes, I know, I don't suppose it seems long since I last did it – we call it an observation – just to make sure everything's as it should be. You know what I'd like you to do, don't you? Have a drink – no, not a proper drink, just a few sips. I know you don't feel like it, but if you get dehydrated you'll be so uncomfortable ... and it helps to keep your mouth fresh. You don't really want me swabbing it out for you when you could be drinking instead. Of course you don't. There, come on Richard, just try, just try. Do it once and it'll be easier next time. I bet you enjoy drinking really. Well, I do. I work in a pub, some nights – did I tell you? It's called The Feathers, not all that far from here. You might have been there, mightn't you? No, we're not supposed to, but I enjoy it. The Guv'nor's a friend of my mum and dad. I prefer nursing though ... of *course* I do. One more sip, Richard, come on, love ... do it for Katy.'

11

'Is he going to get better?' said Elaine.

'If I have anything to do with it – which I do.'

'You're not going to go on about him all morning, are you?'

'No. I thought you wanted to know, that's all. You asked me what I'd been doing,' said Katy, telling herself that by now she should know better than to answer questions like that.

'I should have known better than ask,' said Elaine. 'Well, what do you think of the flat?'

'It's nice,' said Katy. 'Did you choose all the stuff yourself?'

'I didn't choose any of it,' said Elaine, almost proudly. 'I left all that to Chris. An Englishman's home is his castle, he says.'

'That's not exactly an original idea,' said Katy.

'Yeah, but he means it,' said Elaine. '*His* castle.' Three weeks after the wedding Elaine Kingsley, née Bryant, was more heavily married than Katy would have thought possible; but suspecting it she had chosen to pay her visit at a time when she knew the company director would be out, on business; although normal business hours did not seem to apply to him. It was strange how much of his business was conducted in the evenings. Perhaps he too worked shifts, with his shifty friends.

'He knows a fella makes these kitchen units, so *naturally* he chose the stuff to go with them,' said Elaine, gabbling a little. 'I mean, I haven't a clue about furnishing, I mean, I wanted one of those round spin driers but Chris said it would look out of place because the rest of the design was *angular*, so we got a square one.'

'Oh. I thought you were going to have that automatic we looked at; the front loader.'

'We would have,' said Elaine, quickly, 'but this friend —'

'Who makes them?'

'Don't be cheeky, young Betts,' said Elaine, meaning it. A slighting remark about the company director's friends was by proxy a slight on the company director.

'It's only for my things, anyway. Chris sends all his stuff to the laundry.'

'Doesn't he trust you to wash his socks, then?' said Katy.

'He's fussy like that.'

'You're telling me,' said Katy. Even Hughie could never have turned out this bad. Hughie's belief in male supremacy was, after all, mainly theory, all talk. The talk had made Katy uncomfortable, but he had never put it into practice and made her feel inferior, and she was beginning to understand that no one else would ever be allowed to try. The company director had turned it into a full-time job. Oh, Elaine, what's happening to you? 'Are you going to show me the rest of the flat?' said Katy.

Elaine gave her a conducted tour, demonstrating the finer points of Christopher's flair for interior design, from the nasty-minded oil painting over the serving hatch, to the industrial tiles on the bathroom floor, courtesy of another friend. It was like walking on sandpaper.

Towards the end of the display, the Englishman returned to his castle.

'Hullo, hullo, here's Florence Nightingale,' he said, as if he had produced the joke fresh from his remarkable repertoire. He tossed his coat and briefcase to Elaine, who took them away. She didn't get a kiss until the coat was hung tidily on a hanger in the hall cupboard, and then he bestowed one upon her, like a good-conduct medal.

Katy pointed to the second bedroom door. 'Is this going to be the nursery?'

'Billiard room,' said Chris. It was, too. It contained nothing but a half-sized billiard table, a rack of cues and a drinks cabinet full of masculine whisky bottles. 'Men only in here, girls. Eh, Elaine?'

'No nursery?'

'Not likely,' said Chris. 'We're not starting a family, are we, pet?'

'I didn't mean right away,' said Katy, wishing she had said nothing.

'Not right away, not ever,' said Chris the company director. Katy saw that to him this marriage was just one more company; all profit and no loss. 'We don't want kids.'

'Well, you know, I always said I didn't like babies,' said Elaine.

'You might change your mind, later on.'

'Elaine won't change her mind, will you, pet?' said Christopher, implying that Elaine had no mind to change in any case. 'She knows what's good for her.'

Katy left as soon as she could and went to the hospital, where she stood by Richard's bed and held his hand, while antibiotics were administered intrathecally, by lumbar puncture.

If only it was all as easy as holding hands because, without doubt, there was little else that gave so much comfort except, perhaps, morphia.

Mrs Lake came squelching up the stairs to the flat, awash with bad news.

She irrupted into the kitchen, sank down in the nearest chair breathing heavily, her face as lined as a weather map with a depression coming, and gasped, 'Rachel's been taken!'

The whole family froze around the breakfast table.

Taken?

Katy could think only of the Births, Marriages and Deaths page in the paper. *Remembering Rachel, taken 13th November* ... Still, that was better than saying *chosen* as so many of the notices did, as though dying were a reward, conferred for good behaviour.

'Half an hour ago,' said Mrs Lake, with joyous anguish.

'Took where?' said Kevin, who never read the Deaths column, since no one he knew was likely to be in it.

'The hospital,' said Mrs Lake. She saw them relax, unforgivably. 'She's a whole month early!'

'Well, don't worry,' said Katy, equally unforgivably. 'It could be a false alarm. She didn't have a fall, did she?'

'No,' said Mrs Lake, reluctant to admit it. 'But she's in pain.'

'Well, she would be,' said Katy, 'if she's in labour.' She felt herself grow detached and professional, the more melodramatic Mrs Lake became. 'Have the membranes ruptured?'

'What?'

'To release the amniotic fluid.'

'Is that serious?' said Mrs Lake, reviving at the chance of complications.

'Hardly. *You'd* call it "breaking the waters",' said Katy. 'I can look in later to see how she's getting on.'

'This'll be a hard one, she's carrying high,' said Mrs Lake, hopefully. She had never forgiven Rachel for having Jason in the ambulance, without so much as a scream, in ten minutes flat.

'Where's Jass?' said Mrs Betts. 'With Bernard?'

'Bernard's not even home!' shrieked Mrs Lake. This

was the final lovely outrage; an errant husband. 'He's been out all night!'

'He had to take a load up to Carlisle, didn't he? How could he know?' said Dad, who rarely crossed swords with Mrs Lake except when his son's honour was at stake.

'So where *is* Jass?' said Mum. 'Who's got him?'

'He's downstairs in his pushchair,' said Mrs Lake. 'Good thing someone cares what happens to him. He was sobbing his little heart out this morning when she went. I thought Katy might ...'

'Thought Katy might what?' said Katy.

'Well, you're supposed to be so good with little ones. You were in that crèche for a year, weren't you? And I can see you're not going to work ...'

'I'm going to Wandsworth,' said Katy. 'I've got to go before a Board.'

'What for?' Mrs Lake perked up again, imagining that a Board was some kind of court martial for insubordinate nurses.

'I'm going after a job.'

'Oh, if your job's more important than your own family —'

'It is,' said Katy, astonishing herself.

'*I see.* It's just as well his Nanny Lake can —'

'Don't be daft, Winifred,' said Mrs Betts, sharply. 'Katy's not missing her Board to look after Jason. What about the neighbours? Rachel's left him with Mary next door, often enough.'

'I wouldn't leave a cat with that woman. Her eldest's five and he still —'

'All right. He can stay here. Gran will keep an eye on him.'

'Your mother? You'd leave that little boy with a senile old woman all day?'

Mrs Betts stood up, wielding the tea pot. *'Senile?'*

Dad smiled slightly at Katy and jerked his head towards the door. Katy had been hoping that they would wish her luck when she went, but under the circumstances she felt she could manage without, and slipped away before she should actually witness her mother brain Mrs Lake with the tea pot.

When Katy returned to the hospital from Wandsworth, the first person she met was Mrs Lake, churning up the drive like a Chieftain tank.

Mrs Lake looked angry, rather than grieved, so Katy assumed that Rachel was not suffering too much; not suffering enough, in fact, although Katy had no idea how Mrs Lake would act if she were unhappy. She would probably collapse noisily, like a punctured barrage balloon.

'How's Rachel? Has she had it?'

'No, and they won't let me see her,' said Mrs Lake.

How wise, thought Katy. She knew better than to hope that Mrs Lake would ask her how the Board had gone. 'Well, it isn't visiting time, and I don't suppose she really wants to see anyone right now, except Bernard, maybe.'

'I thought hospitals were meant to let mothers stay with their children these days.'

'But Rachel's twenty-three,' said Katy, trying not to laugh. 'It's little babies need their mothers with them.'

'She'll always be my baby,' said Mrs Lake, dabbing her eyes. Katy saw that under the scaly armour Mrs Lake was genuinely upset, if only for herself rather than for Rachel, and was ashamed for not noticing sooner.

'Look, when's Bernard due home? I think you ought to go back and wait for him,' she said, in her most nursey manner. 'He's going to be worried sick if he gets home and finds nobody there, and the neighbours will probably spin him some horrible tale,' she went on, seriously doubting that any neighbour could tell a more horrible tale than could Mrs Lake. 'I'll go and see Rachel in a little while. Don't worry.'

'I'll do that, then,' said Mrs Lake, taking from a nurse what she would never take from her son-in-law's little sister. 'But,' she said, rallying, 'I don't see what he's got to worry about. He's not lying there screaming.'

'I don't suppose Rachel is, either,' said Katy.

'He got her into this.'

'Well, you don't find babies under gooseberry bushes these days,' Katy muttered, moving on. 'Good-bye,' she called cheerily over her shoulder. 'Don't worry.'

When she went along to the maternity ward she found Barbara Marshall, her old ally from the days of Female Surgical, making tea in the ward kitchen.

'Have you got a Mrs Rachel Betts in the labour ward?'

'You're too late, she's had it,' said Barbara. 'Is she a friend of yours? Oh, of course, Betts. I didn't think. Relative?'

'My sister-in-law. How is she?'

'She's fine and the baby's fine,' said Barbara. 'Her mother, however, ought to be put down as soon as possible.'

'Don't tell me,' said Katy. 'Boy or girl? It was premature, wasn't it?'

'A little girl. No, full term. She must have had her dates wrong. Or her mother had the dates wrong. This is her tea. D'you want to take it in?'

Katy took the cup along to the ward and found Rachel propped up in bed looking tired and pleased with herself.

'Here's your tea, Mrs Betts,' said Katy.

'What are you doing here? I thought you were on a different ward.'

'I just dropped in. How did it go?'

'It was easy,' said Rachel. 'Not as easy as Jason, but not bad. I do have some luck, don't I?'

'Barbara – Nurse Marshall – says it was full term. You got the dates wrong.'

'They always say that,' said Rachel. 'Standard practice, hadn't you noticed?'

'Don't tell your mum it was easy – she'll never speak to you again. I ran into her crossing the car park and she was moaning and groaning. I sent her home to look after Bernard.'

'Poor old Bernard,' said Rachel, without much sympathy. 'Have you seen the baby?'

'Not yet. What are you going to call her?'

'Caroline Rosemary Anne,' said Rachel. 'We had it worked out. Raymond Bernard, if it was a boy. We didn't want a boy, really. Now we've got one of each. That's enough.'

'You'd better not tell your mum that, either,' said Katy. 'She wants you to have five, like her. She's hoping for a Caesarian. And you'd better have another think about Caroline Rosemary Anne; you know what the initials spell, don't you?'

Rachel thought about it. 'C.R.A.B. Crab. Oh dear.'

As Katy left the ward Barbara Marshall overtook her in the corridor.

'Are you going down to the canteen? I'm off for lunch.'

'I'll come and have coffee. I don't want any lunch. I had something while I was out, on the way back from Wandsworth. If I get that job I reckon I'd eat there. It was cheaper than hospital food,' said Katy. Now that she was no longer saving she was more generous with herself, but she still objected to money ill-spent. The yoghurt pots were gone from the window sill, although the tea towels were still at the top of the wardrobe. Somehow it seemed unlucky to remove them.

'Wandsworth?' said Barbara. 'Oh yes, you went for a Board, didn't you? How'd it go?'

'Well ...' Katy thought about it. 'It would have gone all right, only I got caught out, didn't I? They had the Sister there, off the ward, and one of the tutors, and the Nursing Officer. The Nursing Officer was one of my regulars.'

'Regular whats?' said Barbara.

'In the pub. You know I work at The Feathers, sometimes? Well, he's often in there – I never knew what he did for a living. He was the first thing I saw when I walked in. That didn't get me off to a very good start.'

'I bet it didn't. What about the rest of it?'

'So-so. I think they wanted someone with more experience; *and* I haven't had my results yet, *and* I've still got to take State finals.'

'So you don't think you've got it?'

'I'm not going to think,' said Katy. 'Time to start thinking when I know. I've got three others lined up already, anyway. One in Birmingham, one in Sidcup and one at the Charing Cross. That's the one I'd like.'

'I've got all this to come,' said Barbara, gloomily. 'How do they expect you to get experience if you can't get a job?'

'It's getting the job that you want that's the trouble,' said Katy. 'I don't want to stay here. I mean, it's not that I don't like St Angela's, but I want to get away from home – and I want to get away from Hughie.'

'I thought that was all over.'

'It is, but he's still *here*, isn't he? And he's all over the place, being a psycho. You never know when he's going to get called in.'

'Surely he's not still on at you to have him back?'

'Not likely. It didn't take him long to find a replacement,' said Katy.

'Not the same ring, I hope,' said Barbara.

'Oh, he's not engaged,' said Katy. 'Just fixed up for the night; you know what I mean? You know he was always on about being a red-blooded male, as though the rest of us had nothing but leucocytes. I bet my Richard's a red-blooded male when he gets back on his feet, but he never talks about it.'

'*Your* Richard? The meningitis case? Aye-aye!'

'You can cut out the aye-ayes right now,' said Katy. 'But I can't help feeling he's a bit special. I was nursing him from the day he was admitted, and now he's in the open ward. I thought we were going to lose him, and he's getting better.'

'Well, he can't do much while he's flat on his back,' Barbara conceded, 'but I bet he's as bad as the rest of them when he's recovered.'

'I don't intend to find out,' said Katy, primly.

12

Rachel and Bernard brought the baby (Caroline Rosemary Jane) round to the flat so that everyone could see her. Behind them paddled Grandma Lake, manhandling Jason and issuing dire warnings about the dangers of exposing little babies to the cold winter air.

'Look, Ma,' said Bernard, wearily, 'the district nurse said she should be in the fresh air as soon as possible. It didn't kill Jason, did it?'

'I saw that district nurse. She was younger than Katy here. Don't tell me —'

'She couldn't have been younger than me,' said Katy. 'It's not allowed. You have to do special training after you've got your finals.'

'What about Jason's asthma?'

'He hasn't got asthma, he's got eczema,' said Bernard.

'You don't get eczema from fresh air,' said Katy, moving to back him up. The whole family became wonderfully united in the presence of Mrs Lake.

The baby began to yell, in a flat, bored voice.

'It's hungry,' said Bernard.

'Don't call her "it", poor little love,' said Mrs Betts, gone frighteningly soft all of a sudden. 'Come to your Gran-Gran while Mummy does your bottle.'

'Let me hold her,' said Joanne. 'Come on, I haven't held her yet.'

Jason decided that he wasn't getting enough attention and dragged the tea tray off the kitchen table. Rachel slapped Jason and Mrs Lake laid into Rachel, partly on

Jason's behalf and partly because she had something to say about young mothers who couldn't be bothered to breast feed their own babies. Rachel began to cry and Katy slid out of the room before they could demand her professional opinion and reject it, meanwhile calling her an upstart for daring to have an opinion at all, especially a professional one.

She went along the landing to Gran's room. Gran also felt that she wasn't getting enough attention and had managed to turn slightly blue round the lips.

'I'm getting that pain again,' she complained, when she saw Katy. 'My chest feels all tight . . . heart . . .'

'It's not your heart,' said Katy, going over to the bed. 'You should have sat up longer after supper, that's all. Look, you've slipped right down in the bed. Come on – let's get you up again.'

'I'm breathless,' said Gran, flapping about with shawls and magazines.

'You're a bit cyanozed,' said Katy, knowing how Gran loved a technical term or two. 'Nothing to worry about. You got enough pillows? Have this cushion.'

Gran was not to be placated with cushions.

'When are they going to bring that baby in? I can hear them all in the kitchen; it's time someone remembered I'm here. I suppose they're afraid I'll drop it.'

'Don't be silly,' said Katy, sadly. This was probably exactly what they did think, especially old mother Lake, so rather than face an argument they had kept Gran out of it altogether. 'Rachel's feeding her at the moment. She's going to bring her in here afterwards. I expect she'd like a bit of quiet herself. It's bedlam in there.'

'She's up too soon,' said Gran. 'They used to keep you lying down for fourteen days afterwards.'

This was a new one from Gran. When Jason was born

Rachel had been in hospital for the full ten days and Gran had never tired of telling them all how she had been back at the wash tub within a week. She and Mrs Lake had enjoyed a splendid set-to seeing which of them could come up with the most miscarriages, borrowing shamelessly from friends and relatives until it seemed that they must have been born pregnant in order to fit them all in.

'They shouldn't have a new-born baby in there with those smelly gerbils,' said Gran. 'Or that canary. You can get parrot disease from canaries.'

Katy wondered that Mrs Lake hadn't thought of that.

'I'll tell Rachel you want to see the baby. She'll bring her in.'

'Rachel's a good girl,' said Gran. Katy went back to the kitchen where Rachel was feeding Caroline and Mrs Lake was recalling a neighbour's infant that had choked to death on a rubber teat.

'Gran wants to see Caroline,' said Katy. 'Will you take her in there when you've finished?'

'Of course I will,' said Rachel, still sniffing a little. 'I'll change her first and then her great-gran can give her a cuddle.'

'If she don't drop her,' said Mrs Lake.

'*And*,' Katy broke in, 'it'd be nice if someone went and sat with her for a bit. She's getting fed up in there on her own, listening to you lot in here. Go on, Jo.'

'Why should I go?' said Joanne. 'It's always me that has to go. What do you think I am, a bleedin' granny-sitter?'

'You'll feel the back of my hand if I hear any more of that talk,' warned Mrs Betts. 'It won't kill you to go in. You can watch telly together.'

'I don't want to watch telly. I got to do my hair. I'm going out in a little while.'

'You get into that room —'

'Why can't Kev? He's not doing anything.'

'I'm going out too,' said Kevin, and precluded any argument by going, since he didn't see the baby as a good reason for staying.

'Why not Katy? She's been sitting around on her backside all evening doing sweet Fanny Adams,' Joanne shouted.

'I got up early to see the baby,' said Katy. 'I've got to go to work in a few minutes.'

'Then you can spend your few minutes with Gran,' said Joanne. 'You always use your work as an excuse.'

'Well if it isn't an excuse I don't know what is,' said Katy, her own voice rising. 'You expect me to work all day and all night and then come home and start nursing all over again. I can't spend all my free time with Gran. It's not fair.'

'It's time you grew up a little then, gal,' Mrs Betts bellowed across the kitchen. 'Not fair! Not fair! You sound like some school kid who can't get her own way. What do you think I do all day while you're off at the hospital? Put me feet up and polish me toenails? I tell you —'

'I just said I didn't see why I should have to do it all when I'm at home. Shifts are hard enough without having to work here as well. No one does anything to make it easier.'

'We'll hire a maid, shall we, Lady Muck?'

'*I'm not sitting with Gran!*' Katy screamed. 'Is that clear? *I'm not going to do it!*'

The baby, rudely aroused from its bottle, began to scream too.

'Now look what you done, you horrible loud-mouthed lot,' cried Rachel, bursting into tears again. Jason, seeing his mother crying, decided to join in. Bernard banged his head on the table. Above the racket Gran's thin voice could be heard wailing, 'I heard that. I heard that!'

Richard Knowles was on the look-out for Katy when she came on to the ward, and beckoned her over to his bed.

'Are you in a hurry?'

'Yes, I am as it happens. I'm about to do the drug round,' said Katy. 'I'll have time for a chat after that – if it's a chat you want.'

'I've been waiting all day,' said Richard.

'I bet.' Katy went away again, reflecting that Joanne's crack about job satisfaction being sore feet and lousy money seemed really cheap when you compared it with the real job satisfaction; which was seeing Richard not only alive but looking it. She knew he was watching her.

When she came back he was ready for her, apparently hiding something under the pillows.

'I don't think I shall see you up here again,' he said.

'It's my last night,' said Katy. 'I go back to Geriatrics on Wednesday.'

'They told me,' said Richard. 'It won't be the same without you. I got you a farewell present.'

'What did you do, nip round the precinct while no one was looking?'

'Don't laugh at me,' he said, as susceptible to insult as he was to infection. He brought out a parcel from under the pillows. 'I'm afraid it's nothing personal. I had to get my brother to buy it for me, and he's not the kind of chap you ask to get personal things.'

'Your brother? The one who looks like he plays for British Lions?'

'He plays at weekends,' said Richard.

'Then I've probably met him – in Casualty,' said Katy.

'I doubt it. He lives in Weybridge,' said Richard. 'Look, take it, for God's sake. I can't stay here waving it all night. Everyone's looking.' He was dreadfully embarrassed. Katy let him get on with it.

'Weybridge? Definitely not the kind we get in on Saturday night.'

'Please take it, Katy.'

'Nurse Betts.'

'Please? It's all right to give you presents, isn't it? It's only chocolates. It ought to be a tiara, but —'

'We aren't allowed to wear tiaras on the wards,' said Katy. 'Can I look?'

'I thought you'd never ask. You don't mind, do you? You will take them?'

'Of course I'll take them. It's ever so nice of you,' said Katy. She didn't tell him what would happen to them.

'I wish it was something more.'

'You don't need to give me anything,' said Katy. She had just looked inside the bag and seen what kind of chocolates he had given her. Taken aback, she stood and smiled at him. The box alone looked like a top-flight undertaker's casket. The chocolates probably had gold fillings. Perhaps that was what you got in Woolworth's, down at Weybridge.

'I'll see you before you go, in the morning, won't I?' Richard pleaded, seeing that she was about to leave.

'You'll see me all night if you stay awake,' said Katy. 'Only you won't, on account of what you just swallowed.'

'Goodnight, then.'

'Goodnight, love.'

'I wish you meant that.'

Oh no you don't, said Katy to herself, as she took the chocolates to Sister's office. You may think you do, but you'd soon change your mind if you'd seen me at home just now. Weybridge, my foot.

Richard's gift provoked some comment next morning when the day staff arrived. Katy had already said goodbye to it as it went to join the rest of the chocolates donated by the grateful relatives and patients, and she was not at all pleased to see it again when Sister Denny called her in to the office, just before she went home.

'I understand that this wedding-cake effort was a present to you, Nurse Betts.'

'Richard Knowles gave it to me, Sister,' said Katy. 'I thought it looked like a coffin, actually.'

'I suppose it does. Curious burial customs they must have round here.'

'Weybridge.'

'That would account for it. Well, as it happens, your name's at the top of the chocolate list. So if you want your coffin – you could have it.'

'Really?' Katy put out her hand to repossess it and then hesitated. 'Does it say what kind they are?'

Sister upended the box. 'Soft centres. Very suitable, under the circumstances. Instant tooth-rot.'

'No teeth where they're going,' said Katy.

'I hope you're not going to give them to a baby, Nurse,' said Sister Denny, severely.

'My Gran. I had a bit of a barney with her, yesterday. She'll like these.'

'So long as they don't remind her too much of her impending end,' said Sister Denny. 'It *does* look like a coffin, doesn't it?'

'I think it's the purple velvet and brass fittings,' said Katy. 'Look, Sister, is it all right if I just go back and let him know I've got them? That old so-and-so in the next bed's been telling him we have to share them. Said one of the porters would probably get mine. He's been rubbing it in and making him feel a fool about it. It's upset him a bit.'

'We don't want him upset, do we?' said Sister Denny.

'*You* haven't been making a fool of him, have you? He's remarkably impressionable.'

'Oh no, Sister,' said Katy, soberly. 'Nothing like that.' She went back to the door of the ward. The curtains were half-drawn around Richard's bed, but there was just enough room for him to see what she was holding as she waved good-bye.

13

Katy began to be occupied with thoughts of examination results, and more than once woke up from a bad dream in which someone had written them in white paint on the tennis court by the nurses' home, with her own name at the foot of the list. Fortunately she was back on Casualty, on nights, which left her very little time to do anything but work and sleep. When she finally heard that she had passed it was a long time before she felt any elation. On the one hand it had seemed impossible that she should pass, because passing was so important. On the other, it seemed equally impossible that she should have failed, because she was good, and knew it. Now it was impossible to think at all. There were still the State finals to come.

Barbara Marshall crossed the canteen to offer her congratulations.

'Have you heard whether you got that job yet?'

'Not yet. I don't think I have, you know. And I'm not even Registered yet.'

'Don't start looking for flies in the ointment,' said Barbara. 'You're half way there. You'll have your badge soon. Don't you go for another Board next week?'

'My fifth,' said Katy. 'Ipswich. I'm working outwards, see. And I'm getting good at answering the questions. "Have you had any experience, Nurse Betts?" "Oh yes, Sister, I'm very experienced at Boards." '

Katy went back to Casualty and walked straight into Hughie, fresh from being kicked by a temperamental emergency case.

'She's taken a great lump out of my shin,' he said, pulling up his trouser leg so that Katy could admire the damage. '"You remind me of someone," she said and Wham! If I hadn't seen her dancing shoes I'd have said she was wearing clogs.'

'Maybe she was a tap dancer,' said Katy. 'Who did she say you reminded her of?'

'She didn't.'

'I expect it was her husband,' said Katy, waspishly. 'Don't tell me you want a dressing on that. Stick a bit of plaster over it.'

'No need to be so short with me,' said Hughie. 'Pax, pax and all that – Latin. It means —'

'I know what it means,' said Katy.

'I understood congratulations were in order.'

'Oh, that. I thought such things were beneath your notice,' said Katy. 'But thanks very much. Come round to The Feathers tomorrow night and I'll buy you a drink to celebrate.'

'Are you still working there?'

'Yes, but not tomorrow night. Dora said I could have the back room, so I'm entertaining. A few old friends and that.'

'And will *he* be there?'

'Who?'

'My successor,' said Hughie.

'Who's been telling you the tale?' said Katy. 'You haven't got a successor.'

'Then we're talking at cross-purposes,' said Hughie. 'What are you celebrating tomorrow night?'

'I passed my finals. What did you think?'

'I understood you were keeping company,' said Hughie, horribly arch, 'with a young man.'

'Is that what you were congratulating me about? I'm

not keeping company with anyone. And I certainly wouldn't lay on a party at the pub even if I was.'

'That's not what I hear,' said Hughie, skittishly.

'Then you've had your ear to the wrong keyhole, mate,' Katy snapped. 'Honestly, Hughie, act your age. You sound like a first-year having a fag and a gossip in the bog while Sister's not looking.'

He wouldn't give up. 'Dallying with the patients, eh, Nurse?'

Katy stared at him in astonishment, and dawning comprehension. 'My godfathers, you really are stupid, aren't you? I mean, *really* stupid.'

'No,' said Hughie. 'I'm not. I thought I'd just put you wise to what some of your little friends are saying. A timely warning.'

'Stupid,' Katy repeated. 'And spiteful. *You* don't care what anyone says about me, but you know I do. I didn't think you'd stoop to repeating lies. You're pathetic.'

'And you're running out of adjectives,' said Hughie, unsure of himself.

'Don't count on it,' said Katy. 'I don't come from a nice home and I didn't go to a good school and learn Latin, but I know a few adjectives that would take your ears off, Sunny Jim, so heave yourself out of here before I remember them.'

Katy dropped into the hairdresser's a few days later and learned that Elaine was no longer working there.

'She left last week,' said the girl at the reception desk.

'She never told me. Is she all right?' Perhaps Elaine was expecting after all. That would be nice: or would it?

'I don't know. I suppose so.'

'I wrote and asked her to my party, but she didn't come. I'd better go round and see her.'

'You better had,' said the receptionist, who didn't care about Elaine or Katy's party. Under the desk she was drawing a moustache on the cover of *Vogue.*

Katy went home and changed. The flat was quiet for once and Joanne was in the living room watching telly with Gran. The coffin was prominently displayed on top of the television set and Gran kept her hearing aid inside it.

Finding that she had the bedroom to herself Katy went to the wardrobe and took down the paper bag with the tea towels in it. For the last time she unfolded them and laid them on the bed; the daisies, the sea-horse, the rose. There was no reason why she should not keep them, or use them, but she didn't want them around any more. They no longer made her feel unhappy. In fact, to tell the truth, she thought they were rather funny; her sole contribution to married life; but for the time being she wanted nothing more to do with tea towels. She put them back in the bag, tucked it under her arm and went out.

The sign below Elaine's bellpush said MR CHRISTOPHER KINGSLEY. There was no mention of Mrs Kingsley. Katy pressed the button and went up the stairs. When she reached the second landing the door was open and Elaine was peering round it.

'Oh, it's you. I thought Chris had forgotten his key.'

'You didn't come to my party,' said Katy, as Elaine stood back to let her in. 'Didn't you get my note?'

'Oh, yes. Congratulations and all that. Chris wouldn't let me come.'

'Wouldn't *let* you come? Why should he care? I didn't invite him.'

'I know,' said Elaine, ruefully. 'I think you hurt his feelings.'

'I didn't know he had any. Hey, I've got something for you.'

'Thanks.' Elaine walked into the kitchen. 'Leave your coat in the hall and come through. D'you want some coffee?'

'Please. Don't you want to know what it is?' Katy shook out the tea towels, rolled them into a bouquet and presented it with a flourish. 'Here y'are, Missus; lovely fresh tea towels.'

'They're nice,' said Elaine. 'Thanks ever so.' She smiled forlornly. 'You know, tea towels was the first thing *I* bought.'

'Oh, you guessed,' said Katy. 'You don't mind, do you? That I didn't buy them specially for you, I mean. I never used them. Where are yours – not those things?' She looked at the plain white tea towels that hung on Elaine's rack; it was just like the one she had wanted for herself, with arms that stuck out of the wall.

'No. Chris got those. He didn't like mine. I got them on holiday, down in Kent. They had little maps on. He said they wouldn't go with the decor.'

'Will he *let* you use mine?' said Katy, with heavy sarcasm.

'Oh, I'll use them, don't worry,' said Elaine. 'I don't have to leave them where he can see them.' She poured boiling water into Christopher's melamine mugs, stirred Christopher's coffee granules with Christopher's spoon and handed a mug to Katy. 'You don't want sugar, do you?'

'No.' Katy sat and nursed her coffee, wondering what to say. Christopher's sunglasses squatted on the table between them, like warders set to watch his wife while he was away. Katy distrusted men who wore sunglasses in December.

'What's all this about you giving up work, then?'

'I've given up work, then,' said Elaine. 'So what?'

'I thought you liked it there. And after all that training ...'

'Chris said he didn't want his wife working. He said people would think he couldn't support me.'

'So you stopped; just like that?'

'Well ...' Elaine wound her fingers together. Her two rings caught the light. 'You know he often comes home during the day. He said he was fed up with coming in to an empty flat. He likes me to be here.'

'And that's all you do all day? Just keep the flat warm for Christopher?'

'He *is* my husband.'

'Is that what you call it? Does he allow you to go shopping?'

'Oh yes.' Elaine laughed, a bit. 'You make him sound like a gaoler.'

'*I* make him sound like a gaoler?'

'He's very good to me.'

Katy stirred her coffee, thoughtfully. 'Personally,' she said, 'I'd tell him to go and tie a knot in his neck and if he didn't jump to it sharpish I'd tie it for him.'

'I believe you would, too,' said Elaine. Katy noticed that she was very heavily made up. Round her jaw the skin looked bluish, through the foundation and powder. She decided to ask no questions about that and contented herself with hoping that it didn't mean what she thought it did.

'I hit my chin on the door, coming in last night,' said Elaine, noticing where her eyes lay. 'I gave it a hell of a thump – thought I'd knocked my teeth loose. Say, did you get that job you went after?'

'At Wandsworth? No, I didn't. And I didn't get the one at Sidcup, or Ipswich, or Charing Cross, or Birmingham. I got picked up on the train coming back from Ipswich, though.'

'I'm surprised anyone dared,' said Elaine.

'It looks like I'll stay on at St Angela's for a bit,' said Katy. 'Not long ago I couldn't wait to get out; now it doesn't seem so bad, somehow.'

'I thought you were mad keen to leave home,' said Elaine. 'So what's changed?'

'Everything, funny enough,' said Katy. 'I think Mum's beginning to understand I can't manage Gran on my own any more. I think the trouble was, I was just a student. She'd got it into her head that I had it easy at the hospital. You know, it was the word "student". She kept thinking of sit-ins and demos and the tax-payers' money going down the drain. Now I've got something to show for it she doesn't mind admitting that I work hard.'

'And what about Hughie?'

'Hughie can chase himself up a gum-tree,' said Katy. 'I mean, he doesn't even upset me any more. I don't feel anything when I see him. He's nothing.'

'You just tell yourself that.'

'No, it's true. He's such a kid, Elaine; you just can't take him seriously.'

'I always said he was a loony,' said Elaine. 'What happened to that other head case you were nursing?'

'Head case? I've never been on Psychiatric.'

'No, *he* wasn't a loony. But you said he had something wrong with his brain. He was on his own, you said.'

'Oh, the meningitis case. Richard. He got better.'

'You smiled when you said that,' said Elaine. 'You don't smile so much these days.'

No more do you, thought Katy. 'Of course I smiled. I said, he got better, didn't I? I thought we were going to lose him. Shall I tell you something?'

'Surprise me,' said Elaine.

'He wrote to me. It was such a nice letter. He said he

didn't want to write to the hospital in case it was opened – what does he take us for? – so he looked me up in the phone book —'

'And rang up all the Bettses?'

'No, he hadn't got the nerve. He got his brother to look up the electoral roll.'

'He's serious?' said Elaine. 'Are you? I thought you said you never went with patients.'

'I don't. You often get asked to make dates for when they get discharged, but you just smile a bit. I never follow them up.'

'But you're going to follow this one up?'

'I never said so. *He's* serious. I haven't done anything except open the letter,' said Katy.

'You going to answer it?'

'I don't know. I don't think I should, but it would be rude not to, wouldn't it? It's such a nice letter.'

'You said. Have you got it on you? Let's have a look,' said Elaine, eagerly.

Once Katy would have shown her and they could have laughed over it together, but this time she shook her head. She felt that Richard still needed her protection and it was not the kind of letter a young man wrote if he thought that it was going to go on display around the town.

'No,' she said. 'I left it at home. Look, Elaine, I got to get back now, but why don't we go to the cinema one evening? Just us. I haven't been to the pictures for ages. Or we could go to a pub.' She acknowledged, guiltily, that she had made the suggestion only to see what kind of a response it got. She was not surprised, therefore, when Elaine shook her head.

'I dunno. Chris takes me out, most nights.'

'Not every night, surely? Tell him you want to go out with me, for once.'

'We'll see. Better not fix anything though, eh, Katy?'

'No. I suppose not.'

'Thanks for the tea towels.'

'That's all right.'

'You'll be round again soon, won't you?'

'Why not? No fear of finding you out, is there?' said Katy. 'Bye-bye.'

As Elaine opened the door to let her out, the heavy tread of the company director was heard upon the stairs. He looked up and saw Katy ready to descend, but being a man of the world felt that it was his place in life to get to the top first. Instead of waiting for him Katy began to run down, gathering speed as she approached him. When he saw that she was not going to stop he had to draw back quickly and she brushed past him, without speaking, but with a well-directed jab from her elbow that could easily have been an accident.

She swung out of the front door grinning, hoping only that he wouldn't take it out on Elaine. Still moving quickly she walked down the road towards Battersea Bridge. In her handbag was Richard's hopeful letter, awaiting a reply.

She could answer it or not, as she chose. It was entirely her own decision.

BOOKS BY ANNE DIGBY IN DRAGON

A HORSE CALLED SEPTEMBER

Mary and Anna were inseparable. They had grown up together, and learned to ride together on Anna's horse September. But then Anna was sent away to school – and Mary had to watch as the horse was crippled with overwork. It was then that Mary decided to embark upon a daring scheme to rescue September. A marvellously exciting first novel.

60p

THE BIG SWIM OF THE SUMMER

Davy wanted Sara to win the big swimming race so he couldn't understand why she was getting mixed up with the strange new girl at Hocking School. Didn't she realize she was throwing away her chances of winning? An intriguing school story that will keep the reader guessing from the first page.

60p

THE ANGELS FIRST AID BOOK, Dorothy Baldwin

Accidents happen all the time: in school, at work, in the home, at play. Would you know what to do if your friend broke a leg or cut an arm badly? Based on the BBC TV nursing series, this book gives simple but essential first aid advice. It is illustrated profusely with photographs (showing nurses from the programme giving first aid) and line drawings.